Winning Ways to Work

Produce Profit and Promotion

Rupert Eales-White

Legend 🔖 Business

Independent Book Publisher

Legend Business, 2 London Wall Buildings,
London EC2M 5UU
info@legend-paperbooks.co.uk
www.legendpress.co.uk

British Library Cataloguing in Publication Data available.

ISBN 978-1-9082480-9-1

Set in Times
Printed by Lightning Source, Milton Keynes, UK

Legend ⓘ Business

Independent Book Publisher

Endorsements

Improving Organisational Performance
"Project Omega [which delivers the improvement within six months of commencement] is research based, intellectually rigorous and honest, well-conceived and creative."
John Vinson, former Director of HR, Chardon Rubber Company, US

Implementing Strategy Effectively
"The content covers, very economically, the important link between strategy and implementation, supported by clear examples, which illustrate Rupert E-W's conclusions."
Brian Baldock, former CEO GUINNESS brewing, Chair of M&S and MENCAP

Providing Useful Tips and Techniques
"This book contains numerous useful tips and techniques for managers and aspiring managers, applicable to any business or organisation."
Brian Edwards, MD (1991-2007) and CEO (2007-2009) of St Ives plc

Focusing on Action
"What I like about this book is that it provides actions that individuals can take to improve their performance. Without action, nothing changes."
Leanne Percy, Manager, Curriculum and Training Services, Australian Institute of Management

Focusing on Behaviour and Goal-setting
"The focus on personal behaviour and the fundamental aspect of setting clear goals provides valuable guidance for us all whatever the stage of our careers".
Miles Templeman, Director General of the Institute of Directors (IOD)

Giving Clear Structure

"I particularly liked the structure of each chapter, which has a nice blend of theory, practical guidance, and case studies. This for me is an excellent recipe for rapid learning and development."
Alan Manning, Head of Human Resources, Fife Constabulary

Developing Effectively

"Contains expert guidance on the development of the manager as an individual, their own team and their relationships with other leaders and managers. The inclusion of a team development programme, based not on theory but on successful experience, is an unexpected bonus."
Alex McPhee, Executive Director of Finance and Corporate Support, East Ayrshire Council

Fulfilling Potential

"A tragedy of business life is the unfulfilled potential that walks away from each workplace, never to return. The success story of business life is the number of people who exceed the expectations of others (and sometimes themselves) by using some under-rated but vital skills to make the most of their potential. Rupert Eales-White writes of these skills in *Winning Ways to Work*."
Jonathan Bond, Director of HR & Learning, Pinsent Mason

Improving Individual Performance

"Results in any organisation are delivered through the performance of its people. Winning Ways to Work provides practical guidance for those who wish to take ownership of their own personal development. No matter what stage they are at in their career, this book has something in it for anyone who wants to improve their performance at work and consequently produce better results for their organisation. It would be a great accompaniment for anyone planning his or her career development."
Alan Manning, Head of Human Resources, Fife Constabulary

Improving Team Performance

"Rupert's principles and approach worked every time across job levels and national cultures. When his techniques have been practiced sufficiently to become habitual, they result in huge leaps forward in creativity and

decision-taking. They also refresh the parts other approaches cannot reach, building strength and confidence for both the team and the individual."
Martin Pexton, former Personnel Director of Allen & Overy, Corporate Development Director of London Merchant Securities, MD of LMS Capital

Improving Leadership Competence
"Contains practical wisdom and psychological insights that together are indispensable to becoming an effective leader."
Miles Emley, Master of the Worshipful Company of Leathersellers, Chairman of St Ives plc (1993-2011)

Further Recommendations
"The presence of a number of witty and contemporary references alongside concise and authoritative advice makes this an enjoyable and rewarding book to read. Key points are easy to identify and understand. This book is an excellent addition to the toolkit of any manager."
Alex McPhee, Executive Director of Finance and Corporate Support, East Ayrshire Council

"Useful and highly readable. People of all levels of seniority can enhance their skills and improve their prospects by taking on board the messages of Rupert's book. "
Jonathan Bond, Director of HR & Learning, Pinsent Masons

The Author
"Draws effectively on a career, rich with experience and learning. Indeed, it is the wisdom acquired from learning which provides strength and authenticity to the key messages the book successfully delivers."
Bryan Smith, Editor, "Industrial and Commercial Training", Emerald Group Publications Ltd; former Director of Studies at Sundridge Park Management Centre

Dedication

This book is dedicated to the memory of my beloved brother Gavin Cushny (né Eales-White). Gavin was a dual citizen of the USA and UK. He was murdered on 11th September 2001 by Osama Bin Laden. Gavin was working on the 104th floor of the North Tower, which the first Boeing hit. Gavin was a man of enormous courage, indomitable will and hunger for life. Though trapped above the Boeing, he nearly broke free from the building. His body was found in a stairwell with another victim and twelve of those incredibly brave New York firemen. He did not die alone.

CONTENTS

FOREWORD

I have always been an avid "self-help" book purchaser. Endless delays at international airports, desperate last minute birthday gifts, and temptation striking during any visit to my favourite book shop, resulting in a mountain of disappointment.

I can count the really helpful publications on a dozen fingers.

The main lesson I take from the many flops is, simply, that the truly outstanding and influential business leader is rarely an effective teacher/coach by way of the written word.

The majority of failed missives suffer from the same characteristics; lack of coherence, poor evidence supporting confident conclusions, impossible navigation for the reader, and a dearth of relevant case studies and practical examples.

I was attracted by the content of Rupert E-Ws book, as it clearly avoided these negatives. The content covers, very economically, the important link between strategy and implementation, supported by clear examples, which illustrate his conclusions.

The focus on the important mix of individual development and team-work is clearly a priority and much under-rated aspect. I saw this as a clear "next-step" from the messages in "Power of Persuasion", an earlier work by Rupert E-W.

Another attraction for me was the focus on self-development.

In my own career, rarely was I motivated to continue personal development outside the classic Personnel Department's Training Department agenda.

I have always felt that coaching is more important than training.

My final comment is to praise the navigation within this book. Succinct summaries and major points of emphasis, clearly and simply stated, are a welcome and unusual value added.

I recommend *Winning Ways to Work* to all managers or those ambitious to become one.

Brian Baldock
CEO GUINNESS brewing, Chair of M&S and Mencap

INTRODUCTION

This book delivers on its title. Set out below are winning ways provided for all employees, managers and executives, and Chief Executive Officers (CEOs).

ALL EMPLOYEES

- Achieve any goal you set yourself.
- Significantly improve all your business relationships through enhanced communication, influencing, persuading, negotiating and creative thinking.
- Improve your ability to be deal with sudden change, initially perceived negatively.
- Think and write with impeccable logic.
- Deliver outstanding presentations.
- Ensure your boss, however "difficult" currently perceived, becomes a champion for your career.

MANAGERS AND EXECUTIVES

- Become a highly effective manager and leader.
- Learn how to build any group of staff into a high-performing team in four hours.

CHIEF EXECUTIVE OFFICERS

- Transform your company's profitability or your non-profit making organisation's ability to achieve its core goals within 6 months of the commencement of the delivery vehicle – Project Omega.

In conclusion, I would point out that you can apply many of the tools and techniques covered in the book in all walks of life. I hope you do, and your life becomes even more fulfilled and rewarding at "work, rest, home and play" than at this moment in time.

Enjoy.

Rupert

Glossary

Term/Acronym	Meaning
"Blood on the carpet"	What poor performing teams operating at the "conflict" level produce.
CEO	Chief Executive Officer
CDMU	Core Decision-Making Unit
"Coming to our senses"	The return to the rational adult ego-state after an attack of the "Hydes" or other SCID
"Commitment" level	The highest performing level of a team, producing synergy.
"Conflict" level	The lowest performing level of a team, producing "negergy".
CS	Communication Style
CSD (Discovered by the author in October 2009)	Critical Strategic Driver. The CSD is the core driver for corporates to increase profitability and hence share price.
Endogenous Shock	A sudden event, perceived negatively, that occurs with a given system, e.g. a team-member making a mistake.
Exogenous Shock	A sudden event, perceived negatively, that occurs outside a given system, e.g. a client "moving the goal-posts" for a team.
GDT (Discovered by the author in August 1992)	Group Discovery Technique, enabling the individual to become more creative and the team to produce synergy.
GSA	Governing Strategic Action – the highest level strategic action that drives a piece of writing with impeccable logic

HR	Human Resources
Iceberg Communication Theory	Up to 90% of our communication, and hence behaviour, is driven from our subconscious
Iceberg's existing three laws of the impact of the subconscious on conscious decision-taking	1. Every stimulus produces a response. 2.A single detail can produce 100% of a . decision 3.You can consciously affect the subconscious behaviour of others and so change their conscious behaviour as a result.
Iceberg's fourth law (Discovered by the author in March 2011)	You can consciously affect the subconscious behaviour of yourself and so change your conscious behaviour as a result.
Keretsu	A nationwide system that enabled Japanese companies to gain a competitive advantage through sharing knowledge and the costs of developing new technologies – hence "zero defects" and "just-in-time" delivery.
MD	Managing Director
M&L	Manager and Leader
MECE	The rule to ensure that your writing exhibits impeccable logic. No point should be duplicated, i.e. Mutually Exclusive, and all answers should be provided to a given question, i.e. points should be Collectively Exhaustive.
Mr Hyde	The biggest beast in the subconscious jungle, causing us to behave hideously or "Hydeously".
"Negergy"	The sum of the creative and decision-making outputs of the team-members exceeds what the team operating at "conflict" level produces
NLP	Neuro-Linguistic Programming society
NSQ	Natural Strengths Questionnaire, determining the natural strengths or bents, with which we are born

PBA rule (Discovered by the author in October 1991)	"Whenever TOP Perceives a Balance of personal Advantage in the proposition you are putting forward, then TOP will say 'yes' to that proposition."
RTB	Rapid Team Builder
SCIDs (Discovered by the author in January 2008)	Subconsciously Controlling Inner Demons. These are negative forces in our subconscious, based on limiting beliefs that drive conscious action without conscious awareness or control, e.g. "Temper Tantrums" or "Road Rage".
SPO (Discovered by the author in April 2006)	Subconscious Psychological Osmosis. This is the process, whereby a given message, if sufficiently repeated in time and over time, "sinks into" our subconscious and progressively seeps into our conscious persona under the conscious radar, so that we form an explicit belief, opinion or viewpoint we consider a "fact of life", e.g. "Expenses Scandal" leading to the belief that all MPs "fiddle their expenses".
Synergy	The creative output and quality of decision-making of the team exceeds the sum of all individual outputs
TOP	The Other Person in a relationship

Chapter 1

Achieve all Your Goals

INTRODUCTION

In this first chapter, we:

- ☐ Start with a case study that demonstrates the need for and power of goal-setting.
- ☐ Consider the role of the subconscious in decision-taking.
- ☐ Consider how you can create a new habit.
- ☐ Advise what actions you should take now to start the process of achieving all your goals.

THE POWER OF GOAL-SETTING

The remarkable 3%

A very powerful piece of research was carried out using Yale University graduates. They were surveyed in the 1950s, when at Yale, and again 20 years later.

The research showed that 3% were worth more in terms of wealth than the other 97% put together. This 3% also had better health and enjoyed better relationships with others.

Only one thing fully explained this remarkable 3%:97% split. It was not parental wealth. It was not degree subjects taken. It was not career selected. It was not ethnicity. It was not gender based. It was not any other of the more obvious factors.

What produced this remarkable difference was that the 3% had produced written goals in the 1950s. The 97% had not.

Clearly, just writing down goals would not guarantee their achievement. To explain what happened, we start by considering the role that the subconscious plays in decision-taking.

THE ROLE OF THE SUBCONSCIOUS IN DECISION-TAKING

The power of "5"

A tutor ran a 3 day development programme for a law firm. Part of the feedback and review sheet asked the delegates to anonymously assess the tutor on a scale from 1= Very Poor to 5= Excellent.

From the opening of any programme to the end, the walls were progressively covered by flip-charts summarizing key information points, key learning points and so on.

On this particular programme (and only on this programme as I put a stop to the experiment when I discovered it), wherever possible and as prominently as possible, the tutor deployed the number 5 and only the number 5, e.g. 5 ways to persuade a client, 5 key learning points, 5 steps to success in negotiation and so on.

It was the only development programme from a suite of programmes that ran for over 13 years, where there was a clean sweep of 5s for any tutor in my tutorial team.

❏　Senior associate lawyers tend to be a somewhat sceptical and cynical bunch. They work themselves into the ground in the hope that they will make partner. They are terrified that they will not make partner. In the absence of the experiment, the programme would have been well received, as the tutor was competent and well versed in the firm's culture. Hardly any 5s would have been given.

❏　What the tutor did was apply the 3rd law of Iceberg communication theory. Let me explain.

ICEBERG COMMUNICATION THEORY

Imagine you are an Iceberg, floating in the Arctic Circle. The conscious communication is what takes place above the surface. The subconscious communication takes place below the waterline. So only 10% of our communication is driven by the conscious self. A massive 90% is driven from the subconscious self. When two Icebergs (people) meet, their initial communication is below the surface, i.e. from the subconscious. "First impressions count". From this reality are derived the three Iceberg laws.

Author's note

I consider the figure of 90% an exaggeration for effect. The actual percentage varies from individual to individual. I have met many individuals who spend most of their time in what is called the "rational adult ego state", i.e. behaving as adults, in full control of themselves and the decisions they take. On the other hand, I have met quite a number of other individuals, where behaving rationally is very much the exception, and the Iceberg percentage would hold true.

1. Every stimulus produces a response

❑　Let us take an example. Introverts with a client-facing role can find themselves in what, for them, are quite nerve-wracking situations. An example would be when they are under a three-line whip to attend a networking event with clients or prospects. They have to join a group of stranger TOPs. (TOP is short for The Other Person(s) in a relationship).

❑　What they fail to appreciate is that one or more members of the group notice them before they speak, either in the act of joining or well before. What they also fail to realise is that their body language as they approach, driven by their fears and worries, conveys precisely that the last place they want to be is where they are and the last thing they want to do is what they are about to do.

❑　This stimulus, driven from the subconscious, produces a negative response from the group of TOPs – again driven from their subconscious. Their reception meets their worst fears. This compounds the problem for the future. It also drives deeper their feelings of inadequacy and low self-esteem. They then start finding all the excuses they can to avoid such painful events in the future.

❑　This means that they do not meet their business development targets. This is a highly career regressive move. It has a negative impact on their performance, image and relationship with their boss. [How the stress can be removed and successful networking achieved is covered in Chapter 4, "Developing Competence in Non-Preferred Areas"]

2. A single detail can produce 100% of a decision

❑ Imagine that you are on the recruitment panel for a company and the panel is faced with two final candidates, who happen to be twins. They are dressed and look identical. They are coming in for the final intensive gruelling. There is a chair placed in front of the interviewers for the interviewee.

❑ The first candidate comes in, and, before sitting down, flicks the cover of the chair and then sits down and says, "Good morning". The second candidate just comes in, sits down and says, "Good morning". Which would you be inclined to choose, assuming you had to make a choice before either candidate had spoken a word?

❑ Everyone goes for the second candidate. However, they reverse the decision if they are told that, in fact, their company is a chair manufacturing one. The candidate's job is to ensure that rigorous quality standards are met. It also changes if they are advised that they have placed a large drawing pin on the chair beforehand to see how the candidates respond!

3. You can consciously affect the subconscious behaviour of others and so change their conscious behaviour

❑ This is what the tutor did to produce the unique clean sweep of 5 = excellent. He used what is termed the process of Subconscious Psychological Osmosis or SPO for short. The repeated message, provided it is unchanged when repeated, impacts on our subconscious and progressively seeps into our consciousness without us being consciously aware. With enough repetitions, our conscious behaviour changes as a result.

❑ The behavioural outcomes are determined by the level of intensity, the degree of repetition and the extent to which a given message is supported by consistent action. There are five that vary from minor to major impact in the following order:

1. We can take a specific one-off action
The example already provided is for the senior associates to give the top mark of 5.

2. We can form a specific fact, viewpoint or opinion
We believe consciously that these "facts", viewpoints, and opinions are our own. We fail to recognize that the source lies elsewhere. Ownership is necessary for our self-confidence. We all like to believe that we are independent thinkers. "We make up our own minds".

3. We can form an explicit belief

❑   Beliefs are very powerful as they drive our thoughts, feelings and perceptions, which combine to drive our behaviours and actions.

❑   A recent example of the power of SPO (Subconscious Psychological Osmosis) and how an explicit belief can be formed is the endlessly repeated message contained in the phrase "Expenses Scandal", i.e. that the behaviour of our MPs is "scandalous". This is now "received wisdom".

❑   In fact, nearly all of them behaved according to well established cultural norms that had prevailed for years. MPs were advised to treat expenses as the salary increase, rewarded by an independent review panel that Margaret Thatcher had denied them in the early 1980s.

4. We can develop an implicit belief

❑   This drives action from our subconscious without conscious recognition of, and hence ability to control, that behaviour. Some of these beliefs are negative, technically called "limiting beliefs". They are our subconscious prejudices, which are never consciously recognised, as that would cause an unacceptable loss of self-image and self-esteem. [There are, of course, many consciously held "limiting beliefs", as in the example above, that all our MPs behaved scandalously, "fiddled their expenses", and many prejudices, e.g. the conscious mutual loathing between supporters of different football teams. Celtic and Rangers have been in the news recently in this regard. There are also many positive, enabling beliefs that can be implicit or explicit].

❑ The implicit limiting beliefs create our "inner demons" or "beasts within". I refer to them as SCIDs, i.e. Subconsciously Controlling Inner Demons. The biggest beast in the subconscious jungle has been given a name by the author Robert Louis Stevenson. His name is (hidden) Mr. Hyde. The implicit beliefs underpinning our Hydeous behaviour are:

– I am the most important person in the world.
– I should control everyone and everything.
– I know everything and everyone else knows nothing.
– I am, in fact, God.

❑ Now, unless we are evil "through and through" (a seamless fusion of conscious and subconscious self), when we are operating in Hyde mode, "men or women behaving badly" (and let's be honest, we all can so behave from time to time), then we do not tell ourselves and everyone else that we are behaving as self-centred control freaks and bullies.

❑ This leads to the first golden reality rule, covering effective relationship management.

GOLDEN REALITY RULE 1
Never ever tell an individual whose behaviour is being driven from the subconscious by hidden Mr Hyde (or any other SCID – Subconsciously Controlling Inner Demon – for that matter) the truth.

❑ The reason is that the SCID owner, being unaware that he or she has been behaving badly, will "shoot the messenger", who is a "dirty little liar". This leads to a temporary and sometimes permanent breakdown in the relationship. [You will discover all the strategies to handle this situation with great aplomb. One very effective strategy is to use "reflective listening", covered in

Chapter 3, "Become a Brilliant Communicator".]

❏ The classic work example is the practical boss who "steals" the ideas of a creative subordinate or direct report, the less pejorative term. This is understandable, as practical people like to manage change very gradually - look back to the past to build carefully to the future and "think inside the box". That is not valued today, in a world full of the mantra of change and the belief that: "change is the only constant".

❏ Today, you need to be an effective change agent and indulge in what practical people consider unnatural practices, e.g. "lateral thinking", "brainstorming", "thinking outside the box", "quantum-leaping", to have an effective career and get to the top. [Chapter 4, "Developing Competence in Non-Preferred Areas", will enable the practical reader to "quantum leap" higher than all creative people and creative people to achieve a new personal best].

❏ So, if direct reports confront their bosses with the "truth of the matter", which is a "hidden truth" for the bosses, they will be shot. They are inevitably seen as "dirty little liars", as consciously, of course, such bosses believe that they came up with the ideas themselves.

❏ The bosses will, at the very least, ensure that a "black mark" is put on the direct report's "dodgy dossier", most employees do not know exist. As bosses are key to career success, these direct reports may find that their careers stall or they become plateaued or, in extreme cases, they are "let go".

❏ In my opinion, all assertiveness training should be abolished and anyone, who is contemplating attending assertiveness training, would be far better served with the much cheaper option of buying and reading this book.

❏ Paul, a senior manager, who attended one such programme, fired up by all his "rights" went back to confront his boss, whose theft of his ideas had become "custom and habit". His company's response was very ingenious.

❏ They carried out a "restructuring" and Paul was sideways moved into a new department. There was only one member of the department – Paul. Very soon afterwards, they carried out a "downsizing". The new department was, "most regrettably", surplus to the new requirements and so the department, in the shape of Paul, was let go. The organisation neatly avoided any unpleasant Industrial Relations dispute for constructive dismissal.

❑   This leads to the second golden reality rule.

GOLDEN REALITY RULE 2
If a boss and a subordinate get into a conflict situation, the organisation will invariably back the boss, regardless of the merits of the case.

[In Chapter 6, "Succeed in the Political World", we set out how you can make any boss, however difficult they are currently perceived, into a champion for your career – without any compromise to your personal integrity]

5. A true aspect of our nature can be pushed into our subconscious to form a suppression or "hidden truth"
See the Sally case study in the next chapter for an example of this.

CREATE A NEW HABIT
In this section:

❑   We look at how a psychologist created a new habit.
❑   Examine the role played by beliefs.
❑   Reveal how the 3% produced their outstanding success.

Author's notes

❑   Research by the Neuro-Linguistic Programming Society (NLP) "proves" that, to turn behaviour into a habit, requires 18 to 20 repetitions. The variation is explained by different personality types – see the next chapter where you determine your personality type.
❑   To achieve success requires a strong belief that it will work, and a high degree of conscious focus and persistence.

THE ROLE PLAYED BY BELIEFS
What is very interesting is the supporting role played by beliefs. It is the

The accepting smile

Madhav, a psychologist, was stressed by any event that was outside his control, e.g. a pile-up on the M25 meaning he was late for work, a boss or client suddenly "changing the goal posts" or the regular criticism he received from his boss.

To eliminate this stress, whenever such an event took place, he said to himself "accept with a smile". It took a lot of effort and repetitions before the internal smile was genuine – rather than a ghastly grimace.

He succeeded, when the internal smile was involuntarily and simultaneously mirrored on his face. It was a very minor smile indeed, a swift wrinkling of the lips that was not noticed by the casual observer.

The first genuine internal smile counted as the first successful behavioural change. After 20 conscious repetitions, it had become a habit. He became a very relaxed, stress free individual – second nature.

message (in this case "accept with a smile") and the accompanying consistent behaviour that dominates the creation of a new habit. The belief that "*I should not devote time and energy trying to change what I cannot control or, at least, influence outcomes in my favour*" tends to be implicit throughout the formation of the habit.

HOW THE 3% PRODUCED THEIR OUTSTANDING SUCCESS

❑   We now have the answers to the 3%'s outstanding success:

– Writing the goals down was key, as this enabled the 3% to have a visual record. I would also guess that they prominently displayed them at home or in the office. They would have frequently read them out loud or to themselves. Necessarily, if prominently displayed, there would have been a form of "subliminal advertising", as was the case with the associates, who all gave the mark of 5.

– The messages would have truly "sunk in". What is more, they would have put some means to achieve the desired end for each goal. There would have been a Madhav type action:

"accept with a smile".

–They would have harnessed the power of positive action. Once repetition of positive action had occurred at least 20 times, their positive behaviours would have become habitual. The positive enabling beliefs would have formed in their subconscious to drive that habitual behaviour on – so that it became "second nature".

PROCESS TO ACHIEVE ALL YOUR GOALS

❏ You can do likewise. This is the suggested process:

– Determine your goals in every area that is important to you – work, key relationships, social, sporting, other hobbies or passions and so on.
– Determine how you would measure success in achieving each, and give yourself a time horizon – a specific deadline by which you will have achieved it. For time horizons more than a year out, it is helpful to set interim milestones.
– Ensure that there is at least one positive Madhav action you identify as being core to achieving the goal. Write the goals, success criteria and actions down on a sheet of A3 paper.
– As "a picture paints a thousand words", start drawing pictures of what success means to you for each goal.
– In the middle of the sheet of paper, write the words, very prominently, "I AM A WINNER".
– Sir Brian Pitman, former CEO of Lloyds TSB, once said to me, "effective strategy requires focus and hard choices". Combining this with "Rome was not built in a day" and "success breeds success", I would start with the goal that has the shortest time frame to achieve and focus all your energies on taking and only taking the actions that will achieve successful accomplishment of that goal.
– Once you have achieved success, you will have generated enormous psychological momentum and can become more ambitious. However, you will be the judge of how far and

how fast you can go after creating this momentum, and you will find the next chapter, in terms of your answers to the Natural Strengths Questionnaire (NSQ) and their meaning, very helpful in this regard.

– Incidentally, it will take time to do all the above, and it will be an iterative process, as you may want to make some changes, in the light of your learning from this book.

– One helpful goal, I suggest you now set, is to have completed the process and filled in your piece of A3 paper within one day of finishing this book.

– You can start by taking and repeating one positive action in a few minutes, and remember to regularly repeat verbally all the content on your sheet of A3, as it comes into being, particularly the phrase: "I AM A WINNER".

CRITICAL CONCLUDING COMMENTS

- What the 3% did, by sheer serendipity, is to apply the 4th Law of Iceberg communication theory, which I discovered a few months ago. *You can consciously affect the subconscious behaviour of yourself and so change your conscious behaviour as a result.*

- You may recall that, earlier in the chapter, I mentioned the development of implicit negative or limiting beliefs, which made us "men or women behaving badly" without being consciously aware of this reality.

- As implied above, what the 3% did, which you can of course do, is to progressively eliminate these implicit limiting beliefs or SCIDs (Subconsciously Controlling Inner Demons) and replace them with implicit positive life enhancing beliefs or SCIAs (Subconsciously Controlling Inner Angels) WITHOUT EVER HAVING TO CONSCIOUSLY ACKNOWLEDGE THE EXISTENCE OF THOSE SCIDS.

- This is an "easy peasy" approach to effective growth and development. Trying to recognise the "dark side" within us can be psychologically painful and frequently damaging, as too much emphasis on the negative can deny the development of the positive.

- Next, I quote the introduction to Chapter 8, "Build an Effective

Team Very Rapidly". *"I have developed a unique recipe - a set of tools, techniques and processes - that creates an effective team in four hours. It has been successfully applied to over a 1000 groups of employees from PAs and night-shift print workers through to CMDUs – Core Decision-Making Units. Many of the groups have had up to 4 different staff levels represented and many have included culturally very diverse individuals."*

❑ It is in the moment of doing this final edit (29th April 2011 – a day that should have some resonance down time) that I have realised that, just like the 3%, with sheer serendipity, I was applying the 4th Law I had not yet consciously discovered, so that the entire focus was "accentuating the positive", ensuring repetition of positive action and hence completely bypassing, necessarily as I did not know individual psychological typology, all the damage created by identifying and accentuating individual difference.

❑ This is the hall mark of conventional team-building, that nearly all these 1000 groups have said produces "blood on the carpet" and teams that generate what I call "negery". This is the opposite of "synergy". "Negergy" means that the sum of the individuals' output, working entirely independently, would have greater than what the malfunctioning team actually produced and the quality of output much better.

❑ Hence, of course, application of the recipe (which I transfer to the reader in Chapter 8) produced universal success, transcending individual, gender, hierarchical, cultural, racial, religious and all other differences.

❑ Finally, on a mildly frivolous note, I conclude with how the application of my 4th law would enable any footballer, whatever their position on the pitch, excluding the goal-keeper, to increase their strike rate "exponentially".

I hate the goal-keeper

If you are a football fan, you may well have noticed that even the most gifted strikers (and all the players in a non-striking role) invariably, when taking a pot-shot at goal (given no time to pause and take a conscious decision), cannot help themselves aiming straight at the keeper.

This is driven from their subconscious, a mindset inevitably formed, given that the goal-keeper is a large human object (dominating the goal area) that moves a lot (catching the eye's attention), whereas the goal-posts are relatively small and don't move at all.

Now, my daughter Sophie is a keen footballer and plays for a team in the Under 16s Surrey League.

I have pointed out this reality to her and suggested that she thinks of any goal-keeper as a dangerous animal, (e.g. a tiger) to be avoided at all costs. She should give any goal-keeper the name of a creature she does not like (does not have to be a tiger – could be a giant spider, ant, rat and so on) and endlessly repeat it – and then always aim a few feet inside the goal-post furthest from the keeper, thus avoiding the fear-inducing or hated object.

I have offered to be the goal-keeper in practice, so that she can harness the power of my 4th law and end up increasing her strike rate exponentially. So far, she has carried out far too few sessions for any change of habit to have taken place.

However, if any footballer is reading this book, then you know what to do to increase your strike rate exponentially (whatever your current position) and become a star in your footballing firmament.

Chapter 2

Play to Your Natural Strengths

INTRODUCTION

"The model underpinning the Natural Strengths Questionnaire (NSQ) is very powerful and robust". *Bryan Smith, Editor, "Industrial and Commercial Training", Emerald Group Publications Ltd; former Director of Studies at Sundridge Park Management Centre.*

In this second chapter:

❑ We ask you to complete the Natural Strengths Questionnaire (NSQ).
❑ Set out the model underpinning the questionnaire.
❑ Consider the impact on business relationships.
❑ Look at the Sally case study – Sally Breaks Free
❑ Conclude by considering how people like to process information.

COMPLETE THE NATURAL STRENGTHS QUESTIONNAIRE (NSQ)

❑ In the table set out below, there are eight sets of activities, marked A through to H. Study each set of activities, starting with A and running through B to H.
❑ You make a decision as to how strongly you like or dislike carrying out each set of activities, taken as a single, complete set. Score 1+ for strong preference, 1 for clear preference, 2 if you are OK with them (you would use them) or 3 if you dislike them (you would avoid them).

❑ You make your decision based on having total freedom of choice. You do not consider whether you carry out any or all of the actions in the work-place, only if you would like to or not, as the case may be.

❑ You choose from one of these four preference rankings for each set, i.e. make 8 decisions. When you have made each decision, you enter your preference ranking in the right hand column.

Author's note
I use the mnemonic TOP throughout, which stands for The Other Party to the relationship.

	Activities	**Preference Ranking**
A	❑ Communicate by talking. ❑ Work out ideas by talking them through with a TOP(s). ❑ Learn through doing and discussing. ❑ Be sociable and expressive. ❑ Maintain a wide and diverse circle of friends and acquaintances. ❑ Express emotions to TOPs. ❑ Be pro-active in a social environment.	
B	❑ Understand the world and the people in it through logic and reason. ❑ Analyse. ❑ Use cause-and-effect reasoning. ❑ Strive for an objective standard of truth.	

Activities	Preference Ranking

☐ Challenge and question to understand and solve problems.
☐ Criticise as a means of getting at the truth and expect TOPs to accept it impersonally.

C

☐ Focus on what is real and factual.
☐ Be factual and concrete.
☐ Improve existing structures and systems, i.e. "think inside the box".
☐ Ensure things have a useful and tangible benefit to yourself and TOPs.
☐ Build carefully and thoroughly towards conclusions.
☐ Understand ideas and theories through practical applications.

D

☐ Plan and schedule many areas of your life.
☐ Have things decided.
☐ Allow plenty of time to plan and focus to avoid the stress of last-minute deadlines.
☐ Be methodical and systematic.
☐ Follow routine and use tried and tested methods.
☐ Make short-term and long-term plans.

E

☐ Communicate in writing.
☐ Work out ideas by reflecting on them on your own.

Activities	**Preference Ranking**

    ❏ Learn in a quiet setting with extended mental reflection.
    ❏ Be private and contained.
    ❏ Maintain a small circle of close friends.
    ❏ Express emotions within yourself.
    ❏ Be reactive in a social environment.

F   ❏ See relationships as the source of meaning and truth in life.
    ❏ Empathise.
    ❏ Assess impacts of decisions on people.
    ❏ Strive for harmony and positive interactions.
    ❏ Incorporate diverse viewpoints into compromises that satisfy as many TOPs as possible.
    ❏ Be kind and tolerant towards TOPs and expect them to respond in the same way.

G   ❏ Focus on patterns and meanings in data.
    ❏ Be imaginative and innovative.
    ❏ Generate new concepts and structures, i.e. "think outside the box".
    ❏ Consider possibilities and what might be rather than what is.
    ❏ Move quickly to conclusions, following hunches.
    ❏ Want to clarify ideas and theories before putting them into practice.

	Activities	Preference Ranking
H	❑ Make decisions on the spur of the moment, "go with the flow". ❑ Keep things loose and open to change. ❑ Work with imminent deadlines as they generate most creativity and energy. ❑ Be open-ended and casual. ❑ Have variety and the freedom to decide what tasks you will do when. ❑ Adapt, change course.	

THE MODEL

In this section, we:

❑ Make some initial key points.
❑ Look at the model as a whole.
❑ Consider the four key areas or dimensions to life.

KEY POINTS

❑ The model has been developed by integrating and simplifying relevant aspects of the work of Carl Jung on psychological types, Eric Fromm on life orientations, Ned Herrmann on whole brain dominance and Dr Kirton on adaptive and innovative cognitive thinking styles.

❑ The 8 sets of activities are referred to as natural strengths, dispositions, preferences, proclivities, bents or orientations. The combination indicates what type of person you are. Hence the phrase that we can stay "true to type" or behave "atypically".

❑ A score of 1 or 1+ is called a dominance. If you have a score of 1+, there are two possible implications:

1. Your current role does not allow you enough opportunity to play to these strengths, which causes a degree of frustration and stress.
2. Your current role allows you to deploy these strengths fully. There is the danger of excessive use, i.e. "strength into weakness".

❑   A score of 3 is called an avoidance. If you have a score of 3, there are two possible implications:

1. In normal circumstances you would have given a score of 2, but the demands of the job mean that you have to deploy these activities excessively – causing a degree of stress.
2. Your job does not require excessive use, which means that this set of activities form a weakness or area for development.

THE MODEL AS A WHOLE

Key Area or Dimension	One preference	The other preference
Gain energy	A= External Obtain energy from and focus on the outside world of	E = Internal Obtain energy from and focus on the inner world of thoughts, ideas and experiences.
Natural disposition	people and activity. Extroverted	Introverted
Produce ideas	C=Adaptively Adopt a practical approach, focus on the facts and what is real	G= Innovatively Focus on concepts, see the big picture and work out the relationships and connection between facts.
Natural disposition	and tangible Practical	Innovative
Make decisions	B=Logically Take a detached, logical approach,	F= Harmoniously Consider what is important to self and TOPs affected by

Key Area or Dimension	One preference	The other preference
	examine the pros and cons, evaluate and analyse to reach a fair and reasonable decision.	the decision or involved in the decision-making process, aim for a result that creates harmony and show respect to all TOPs concerned.
Natural disposition	*Control*	*Care*
Operate in the outside world	**D= In an organised way**	**H = Flexibly**
	Take an organised, planned and structured approach.	Be flexible and spontaneous; remain open to new information and last minute options.
Natural disposition	*Organised*	*Flexible*

THE FOUR KEY DIMENSIONS

In this section we look at each of the four key areas or dimensions to life and make some relevant points to develop and clarify the model.

Extrovert/Introvert

❑ Society consists of a very large number of groups of individuals, varying widely in size and power. Each group engages in a number of activities driven by a shared sense of purpose or common cause. Society, by definition, is an extrovert.

❑ As a result, most extroverts do not recognize that introversion exists. Such extroverts judge introverts and behave towards them as if they were extroverts. Specifically, they:

1. Label introverts as antisocial for slipping away to have quality time on their own, they need to recharge their batteries, or for ducking out of networking or social events.

2. Interrupt introverts to have little chats the introverts want to avoid.
3. Dominate meetings so that the introvert's voice is not heard and so their insights do not see the light of day.

Practical/Innovative

❑ Whilst practical and innovative people are both creative, their approach to creativity is fundamentally different. Let us examine a helpful definition of change, i.e. "making or becoming different".

❑ "Becoming different" requires "continuous improvement", where you move gradually from the past into the future, avoiding discontinuity. This is fertile ground for the ideas from practical people – "thinking inside the box".

❑ "Making different" requires discontinuity and quantum leaps, fertile ground for the ideas of innovative people – "thinking outside the box".

❑ Innovative types are often labelled as being the creative ones. Practical types are often labelled as having little or no creativity. As we now know this labelling is wrong. This is why I use the word "innovative" rather than "creative".

❑ Proving this point has been the life-time work of Dr Kirton, who is very practical or, to use his terminology, was born with an "adaptive cognitive thinking style".

❑ As someone who is naturally innovative and "enjoyed" the incredibly detailed, 4 day certification programme twice, I know the truth of the saying "there is no gain without pain". I would like to add the word "considerable" before "pain"!

Control/Care

❑ It is clear when you read the list of activities that those that aim for harmony in decision-taking are caring types. It is not immediately obvious that logical decision-makers are controlling types.

❑ When logical decision-makers are in a rational or "adult" state, they use a *"detached, logical approach, examining the pros and cons, evaluating and analysing to reach a fair and reasonable decision"*.

❑ However, when logical decision-makers become emotionally involved in the decision, they move from the adult state into what is termed the controlling parent state. Their focus of attention moves from obtaining the truth, to themselves, i.e. they become self-centred. In short, they become irrational and their agenda is to get their own way – to win for themselves. Their conscious behaviour is governed by a hidden Mr Hyde.

❑ In their drive to get their own way, irrational controllers become aggressive and use "twisted" logic, i.e.

– Adopt an arrogant, condescending tone of voice, treating you as a mentally retarded three-year-old.

– Mount a sustained attack on your opposing point of view.

– Very unhelpfully introduce points you have not made as the key plank of your own argument. They then destroy these points with consummate ease. They, of course, only introduce points that they can rebut with masses of evidence. You become angry at this totally untrue and unfair "twisting", playing straight into their hands, as the last thing they want is for you to remain calm and rational or "cool".

– Invariably introduce early on, as part of the cunning, subconscious distraction strategy, some fault you have, which is completely irrelevant, or some behavioural incident you have already apologised for (a couple of million times). This is to reduce your self-esteem from the dizzy heights of a mentally retarded three-year-old to the depths of a slowly dying crushed slug.

– Only bring into play opinions, presented as facts, which support their position. Crush any counter arguments by this twisted logic (driven by self-centred emotion and not the facts and so requiring the facts to be "twisted").

– Frequently, they will create new "facts", more accurately referred to as "lies".

– If that fails, shout you down.

– If that fails, stomp off, claiming victory.

❑ There are two triggers that cause a rational controller to move into an emotional self-centred state:

1. When the rational discussion is leading to a conclusion which is not perceived, subconsciously, as in the controller's best interests.
2. When TOP becomes emotional in their support of "others" (not the controller) affected by the decision. If TOP is a carer, then the "others" are other people, affected by the decision. If TOP is a controller, the "other" is themselves.

❑ When a carer is confronted by an aggressive, highly emotional controller, their natural desire to put others first overwhelms them. Specifically, they defer to the controlling parent and lapse into the passive child state. They turn into "worms" – lose confidence and self-esteem, and blame themselves.

❑ When two rational controllers are in rational debate and one becomes irrational and aggressive, typically we have the office equivalent of "road rage". Two stags lock horns and there is a blazing row. Assuming one stag is the boss and the other a subordinate, any "blood spilt on the carpet" will be the subordinate's. Having a blazing row with your boss can be more than simply "career regressive". It can be "career terminal", as we know.

❑ As mentioned in the previous chapter, the technique in Chapter 3, "Become a Brilliant Communicator", entitled "listen reflectively" will not only ensure that you never have a row with an irrational controlling boss, but that you will become his or her favourite in the work-place.

Organised/ Flexible

❑ Social and business norms and conventions are that you should get to meetings and events on time, meet deadlines, and plan for events that involve a group of people. Hence the well-known phrase, "born organiser."

❑ Flexibles often find they receive the following comment during the annual appraisal: *"Your time management is poor and you consistently miss deadlines. I have arranged for you to attend a course on effective planning and self-organisation".*

❑ Flexibles can be made to feel guilty at their behaviour, which creates stress.

❑ There is no phrase in our language, "born flexible", (when referring to basic psychological types!) as it is seen as "politically incorrect" behaviour. Flexible behaviour is, in fact, in increasing demand in our world where "change is the only constant".

❑ It is, of course, very helpful to any individual, if they can learn to get the "best of both worlds". This holds true across all four dimensions and highlights the value of Chapter 4, "Develop Competence in Non-Preferred Areas."

THE IMPACT ON BUSINESS RELATIONSHIPS
We start with a case study

We are soul-mates

James was an English city banker, based in London. He had recently become engaged to Li Han, a Malaysian Chinese, born and bred in Ipoh. James' parents had put him under enormous pressure not to get married because of the differences in race, culture and upbringing.

He was determining his natural dispositions along with the rest of the delegates on a development programme. At the same time as he was determining his own set of natural dispositions, he was determining Li Han's.

At the end of the process, James had a Eureka moment. He exclaimed out loud to the group, "Li Han and I have identical profiles – we are soul-mates."

❑ This demonstrates the power of nature over nurture. There are two conclusions:

1. Like attracts – those with the same set of dominances/natural preferences are attracted to each other.
2. Opposites repel – those with an opposing set of dominances/natural preferences dislike each other.

❑   To illustrate this second point, we will imagine that George is extroverted, practical, controlling and organised. Fatimah is George's boss and is introverted, innovative, caring and flexible. If we take but one activity from each opposing dominance, we have the following:

George
❑   Expresses his emotions to Fatimah.
❑   Builds carefully and thoroughly towards conclusions.
❑   Criticises Fatimah as a means of getting at the truth and expects Fatimah to accept it impersonally.
❑   Allows plenty of time to plan and focus to avoid the stress of last-minute deadlines.

Fatimah
❑   Keeps her emotions to herself.
❑   Moves quickly to conclusions, following hunches.
❑   Is kind and tolerant towards George and expects George to behave in the same way.
❑   Works with imminent deadlines as they generate most creativity and energy.

❑   More generally, those with opposing dominances/natural preferences have opposing beliefs and values, and use language and phrases that are fundamentally different. We illustrate this by setting these out for each of the four dimensions.

Author's note
You can have a dominance that is not a natural preference, because of suppression – see Sally case study in next section.

Extrovert
Believe in/value

Social interaction, conversation, networking.
Words
❑   Talking, discussing, doing, sociable, expressive, networking,

Introvert
Believe in/value

Peace and quiet, contemplation, one-on-one relationships.
Words
❑   Writing, reflecting, quiet, private, contained, peace,

Extrovert

sociable, expressive, networking, interaction, emotions.

Phrases

❑ I am a people person; this is a networking opportunity; I am a social animal; let's chew the cud together; let's brainstorm this issue; I just want to pass this one by you.

Introvert

private, contained, peace, contemplation, one-on-one relationships.

Phrases

❑ I am sorry, I am too busy to chat; I am sorry, I must work on my own this evening to meet the deadline (to avoid pressure to attend a social or networking event); I must have some peace and quiet to concentrate; voice mail "I am out at meetings all morning" (having booked a meeting room to work on their own that morning); I will be working from home tomorrow to get the project completed on time. *Note:* These tend to be reactive phrases, because of extroverts treating introverts as if they were extroverts.

Practical
Believe in/value

❑ Common sense, the tried and tested, traditions and conventions, personal comfort and security, risk avoidance, the present.

Words

Practical, factual, efficient, keep, concrete, cautious, adapting, improving, building, thorough, common sense, security, traditions, risk avoidance, the present, adaptive, mission.

Innovative
Believe in/value

❑ The need for change, originality, taking risks, variety, exploration, the future.

Words

Concepts, patterns, imaginative, innovative, possibilities, quickly, hunches, originality, variety, taking risks, exploration, the future, creative, vision, change.

Practical

Phrases

❑ Look before you leap; stuck in the mud; risk avoidance; safety first; we should learn from the past; we must do a risk analysis; I need a thorough briefing; the devil is in the detail.

Innovative

Phrases

❑ Nothing ventured nothing gained; quantum leap; risk-taking; head in the clouds; change is the only constant; see the big the big picture; our vision.

Logic/Control

Believe in/value

Logic, rights, reason, fairness, rationality, reasonableness, firmness, criticism.

Words

❑ Logic, reason, analyse, evaluate, objective, criticise, rights, fair, intellect, appraisal.

Phrases

❑ IQ, cause and effect; the facts speak for themselves; the one right answer; objective truth; I am a reasonable person; my mind is made up; it's only fair and reasonable, firm leadership; strong management; staff are our greatest asset; human resource.

Harmony/Care

Believe in/value

Harmony, mercy, feelings and relationships, tolerance and gentleness, compassion.

Words

❑ Harmony, relationships, respect, empathy, interaction, compromise, tolerant, feelings, values, feedback, responsibilities.

Phrases

❑ Smile and the whole world smiles with you; wearing your heart on your sleeve; emotional intelligence; supportive leadership; customer care; client service; client delight; supporting our values; learning opportunity.

Organised

Believe in/value

"Failing to plan is planning to fail", structure, routine, organisation, tried and tested methods, orderliness, closure on decisions.

Flexible

Believe in/value

"The plans of mice and men gang aft agley", flexibility, spontaneity, variety, change, freedom, choice.

Organised	**Flexible**
Words	*Words*
❏ Organised, plan, schedule, structure, methodical, systematic, routine, method, order.	❏ Flexible, spontaneous, casual, open, variety, choice, options.
Phrases	*Phrases*
❏ Failing to plan is planning to fail; I need closure on this one; tried and tested; project schedule; signed, sealed and delivered; it's a done deal; short term plan; long term plan.	❏ The plans of mice and men gang aft agley; going with the flow; I'm keeping my options open; open-ended; spur of the moment; multiple choice; freedom to choose.

Key point

Chapter 6, "Succeed in the Political World", sets out all the strategies to ensure you have effective relationships with all TOPs in your business world, to be seen as "one of us" rather than "one of them".

SALLY BREAKS FREE

❏ If, as children, we have a message consistently given to us over a prolonged period of time, especially if it is reinforced by consistent action, we can suffer, without any conscious awareness, the suppression of a true aspect of our nature to form a "hidden truth". This is the deepest level of penetration, level 5, already covered.

❏ We provide an example of the power and the benefits of conscious recognition by using the Sally case study.

Sally breaks free

Sally, a university graduate aged 22, decided she wanted to have a career in Personnel. She joined a large organisation as an assistant training officer. She was very competent, performed very well and was promoted to training officer at the end of her first year.

However, she found that the work she did became increasingly stressful. She started to drink on her own, felt very guilty, but could not break this new habit. She also took up running 10ks.

To prepare her for her next promotion, she was sent on a management development programme. During the course of this programme, she completed the NSQ and received 1 to 1 feedback. This feedback enabled her to eliminate her stress and transformed her career.

Key Points

❑ Sally was born an introvert – her natural disposition in this key dimension. However, both her parents were extroverts who did not realise introversion existed. They, therefore, consistently and repeatedly punished anti-social ("introverted") behaviour. They also promoted and repeatedly rewarded extroverted behaviour.

❑ When Sally became a young adult, she consciously saw herself and behaved as an extrovert. Her true introverted nature had been suppressed into her subconscious. It had become a "hidden truth".

❑ Most of her actual work was running on-site seminars or off-site development programmes most days of most weeks, as the trainers were rushed off their feet. This was very extroverted activity – excessive and caused Sally stress.

❑ Additionally, on many occasions, many of the participants were resentful at being "sent" on the particular seminar or programme. Whilst Sally handled the situation well, it caused her even more stress. Being a natural introvert, she had to spend most of the time using coping strategies (e.g. putting on a bit of an act).

❑ Her true introverted nature grew more powerful as time passed – struggling to break free. *"Nature and the hidden truth will out"*. Hence the destructive drinking on her own and the constructive 10k running – the much needed "loneliness of the long distance runner".

❑ The most stressful thing for Sally is that she did not have a clue as to why what was happening to her was happening to her.

❑ Now Sally gave herself a score of 1 in Extrovert and 2 in Introvert. You can have a dominance that is not a natural preference. During the course of the feedback and discussion session, she discovered the cause and the effect. This was a Eureka moment for her.

❑ Sally had another Eureka moment a little while later. When Sally was born, the prevailing social norms were that men were the controllers – sole bread-winners and masters of the household. Women were the carers – supported their husbands and raised a family. Sally's father was a very dominant controller, who held the belief that women should be carers. Sally was born a controller but raised a carer.

❑ Her father harnessed the power of SPO. This was not a deliberate conscious act, but the result of his strongly held views. By the time Sally left home, she saw herself and behaved as a carer, with her natural controlling nature suppressed into her subconscious – another "hidden truth".

❑ The combination of suppressions led to her "choices" – working in an extroverted environment in an extroverted role in the caring part (people development) of the caring side (personnel) of business.

❑ Incidentally, Sally's scores were 1 in control and 2 in care – again confirming the point that you can have a dominance that is not a natural preference. Again, the 1-to-1 feedback session promoted discovery of this truth.

❑ At the end of the programme, Sally completed her 10 year plan. She was a "born organiser". She achieved it in 9 years and exceeded her initial expectations. She was aged 25 when she formulated the plan.

– Aged 25, she was promoted within her organisation to manager, graduate recruitment:
– Aged 27, she was promoted to senior manager, Personnel.
– Aged 29, she moved to a smaller organisation in her sector as Personnel Director.

– Aged 31, she left to set up her own recruitment and selection business.

– Aged 34, she was making four times the amount she was making as Personnel Director.

Author's note
She plays to her natural strengths. There is never any danger of excess, as she has lived in and operates effectively on the, "dark sides".

PROCESSING INFORMATION

❑   This is the icing on the NSQ cake. In this section, we focus on the key essentials of Neuro-Linguistic Programming (NLP).

❑   There are three primary ways we absorb and process information :

1.   Through our eyes – Visual.
2.   Through our ears – Auditory.
3.   Through our feelings – Kinaesthetic.

❑   Individuals tend to have one preferred method of absorbing and processing information. We look at the characteristics of each type:

VISUAL
People strong in the visual processing function memorise and learn by pictures, diagrams and videos. They have trouble remembering and get easily bored by long verbal dialogue as their minds tend to wander. They are very interested by how things look and less distracted by noise than others.

AUDITORY
People strong in the auditory processing function can repeat things back easily, learn by listening and explaining to others. They like music, talking on the phone and the sound of their own voice. The tone of voice and choice of words used are very important. They are easily distracted by noise.

KINAESTHETIC

People strong in the kinaesthetic processing function memorise by "doing" and respond to physical rewards and touching. They like to walk it through and are interested in if it feels right – like to follow their "gut feelings".

❑ Individual preferences are revealed by the words and phrases used as per the following table:

Processing function	Words/Phrases
Visual	❑ I see what you mean. ❑ Can you cast some light on it? ❑ Paint me a picture. ❑ Let's look at the big picture. ❑ I am looking closely at the idea. ❑ Beyond a shadow of a doubt. ❑ The problem keeps staring me in the face. ❑ That puts things in a better perspective. ❑ That really brightens up my day. ❑ Having your head in the clouds. ❑ Every cloud has a silver lining.
Auditory	❑ I hear what you're saying. ❑ Doesn't ring any bells with me. ❑ I'll give you a bell. ❑ Turn a deaf ear. ❑ Can I bend your ear? ❑ Music to my ears. ❑ It suddenly clicked. ❑ I hear you loud and clear. ❑ That sounds great. ❑ He's constantly giving me static about that. ❑ That guy is really off-beat. ❑ Bring to a grinding halt. ❑ The solution was screaming out at me.

Processing function	Words/Phrases
Kinaesthetic	❑ Trust my instincts.
	❑ Gut feeling.
	❑ Feel it in my bones.
	❑ Get in touch with me.
	❑ I can grasp the concept.
	❑ Hold on a minute.
	❑ I can't quite put my finger on it.
	❑ I am absolutely immersed in this project.
	❑ The pressure's on/off.
	❑ The concert was really hot.
	❑ That guy was a slime ball.

KEY POINTS

❑ You can increase your empathy with a TOP by picking up the primary processing function and speaking in the same language.

❑ If you are called upon to make a presentation to a group of people, then you can guarantee that all processing preferences will be present. You therefore need to:

– Ensure the presentation is clear, concise and to the point. This is covered in Chapter 5 – "Think and Write with Impeccable Logic". This will involve your Auditories and stop your Visuals getting bored.

– Add images that connect directly to the key text messages. "A picture paints a thousand words". This will involve your Visuals.

– Speak with as much passion and commitment as you can muster. This will involve your Kinaesthetics.

– Ensure that, when speaking to your slides, you use the language of all three primary processing functions. This will involve all three types.

Author's note
In Chapter 5 we provide a complete guide on how to make outstanding presentations.

Chapter 3

Become a Brilliant Communicator

INTRODUCTION

To be a brilliant communicator, we need to be able to:

❑ Demonstrate "cool" behaviour.
❑ Ask the right question.
❑ Listen effectively.
❑ Listen reflectively.
❑ Negotiate successful outcomes for both parties – win/wins.

DEMONSTRATE "COOL" BEHAVIOUR

❑ We start by looking at the three factors that contribute to effective communication. These are what we say, how we say it, and our body language. The table below sets out what constitutes each factor and the percentage contribution to effective communication.

Factor	Description	% Contribution
What we say	❑ Actual words used	7%
How we say it	❑ Tone of voice – cold through to warm ❑ Inflexion – way the tone changes ❑ Pitch and emphasis ❑ Speech patterns – fast, slow, hesitant ❑ Use of pauses	38%
Our body language	❑ Use of the eyes – the window to the soul ❑ Gestures ❑ Body posture	55%

KEY POINTS

❑ With body language at 55%, we can see how important it is to adopt a body language that is appropriate to the situation we face. That is why explorers seeing tribesmen advancing on them with spears raised made themselves look smaller, put a broad smile on their faces (instead of the rictus of fear that would naturally appear) and advanced slowly and humbly with both hands palms up to demonstrate the absence of any weapon.

❑ The implications for effective communication vary according to the type of communication deployed. We look at:
 – Face to Face
 – Telephone
 – E-mail

FACE TO FACE

❑ The three main types of behaviour are:

– Passive behaviour.
– Assertive behaviour to which we will refer to as "cool" behaviour, because the word "assertive" can overemphasise the ego, and grate on the receiver's subconscious – "I, I, I".
– Aggressive behaviour.

❏ The table below sets out the 93% for each type of behaviour, separating out into:
– Voice
– Speech
– Eyes
– Face
– Body
– Feeling

	Passive	Cool	Aggressive
Voice	❏ Sometimes wobbly ❏ Tone may be singsong or whining ❏ Over-soft or over-warm ❏ Quiet, often drops away at the end	❏ Steady and firm ❏ Tone is middle range and warm ❏ Sincere and clear ❏ Not over-loud or quiet	❏ Very firm ❏ Tone is sarcastic, sometimes cold ❏ Hard and sharp ❏ Strident, often shouting, rise at end
Speech	❏ Hesitant and filled with pauses ❏ Sometimes jerks from fast to slow ❏ Frequent throat-clearing	❏ Fluent, few awkward pauses ❏ Emphasizes key words ❏ Steady, even pace	❏ Fluent, few awkward hesitancies ❏ Often abrupt, clipped ❏ Emphasizes blaming words, often fast

	Passive	Cool	Aggressive
Eyes	❑ Evasive, looking down	❑ Firm but not a "stare" down	❑ Tries to stare down and dominate
Face	❑ "Ghost" smiles when expressing anger or being criticised ❑ Eyebrows raised in anticipation (e.g. of criticism) ❑ Quick changing features	❑ Smiles when pleased, frowns when angry, otherwise open. ❑ Features steady, not wobbling ❑ Jaw relaxed, not loose	❑ Smile can become awry, scowls when angry ❑ Eyebrows raised in amazement/disbelief ❑ Jaw set firm, chin thrust forward
Body	❑ Hand-wringing ❑ Hunching shoulders ❑ Stepping back ❑ Arms crossed for protection ❑ Covering mouth with hand ❑ Nervous movements which detract (shrugs and shuffles)	❑ Open hand movements (inviting to speak) ❑ "Measured pace" hand movements ❑ Sits upright or relaxed (not slouching or cowering) ❑ Stands with head held up	❑ Finger pointing ❑ Fist thumping ❑ Sits upright or leans forward ❑ Stands upright "head in air" ❑ Strides around (impatiently) ❑ Arms crossed (unapproachable)
Feeling	❑ Guilty	❑ Confident	❑ Angry

As regards the verbal component, the received wisdom is that you combine "I" statements with the "broken record". Looking at each in turn:

"I" statements

When communicating assertively or "coolly", received wisdom is that you use the first person, e.g. "I need you to get to work on time", rather than being impersonal, e.g. "Would you please get to work on time." Whilst you should not lay the source of the request elsewhere, "the boss wants you to get to work on time", or "it is company policy that you get to work on time", or "according to your job description, you have to get to work on time", the direct use of "I" can, as mentioned, grate on the recipient's subconscious, especially if repeated. An impersonal statement, therefore, is to be preferred.

The broken record

❑ The "broken record" means that you simply, in a calm, confident manner, i.e. "coolly", repeat the particular statement (without altering the words used one iota) as many times as it takes, until you get the desired "Yes". You will always be effective, provided you completely ignore any excuse or reason given for the bad behaviour, i.e. do not get distracted by, "red herrings".

❑ It is an example of the power of Subconscious Psychological Osmosis (SPO). The repetition of the same statement operates through TOP's subconscious to produce the conscious agreement: "Yes, I will get to work on time in future."

❑ Typically, three times does the trick – the power of 3. Only once, in my personal experience, did it take more – five times to be precise, and that was with an individual, who had completely lost his cool.

– The three times rule generally holds for a single piece of information or request. Clearly if the message requires a new belief to come into place, then the repetition has to be much more frequent.
– If you use "I", although the power of SPO means that the individual gives away, there is a dislike of the person using the "I"

building up in TOP's subconscious, which perceives a desire to dominate and be in control.

– So always be impersonal, whether with a work colleague, spouse or child. We have the example, where, without changing the actual words used, you repeat the polite request: "Would you please get to work on time" or "Would you please stop hitting your sister" with a child or whatever.

– The key is to develop, through plenty of practice, a range of tones of voice from the "quiet and warm "(almost always to be used in the work-place) to a very firm, cold, consciously controlled, authoritative, raised (but not a shout) tone of voice - very helpful with a recalcitrant child.

TELEPHONE

❑ With the 55% body language gone, then the actual words contribute 18% and how we speak a massive 82%, as to how effective we are when talking on the telephone.

❑ Many years ago, there was an experiment. One set of sales-people carried out their normal "professional" approach. The others were told that, before they talked to the prospects, they had to have a genuine smile on their faces. That genuine smile generated warmth in the tone of voice that resulted in significantly greater sales than the "professionals".

❑ So, if you want to have an effective telephone conversation, then come across with as warm a tone of voice as you can.

E-MAIL

❑ With e-mails (and any form of written communication), the words we use, which contributed a miserly 7%, now take up the entire 100%. Theoretically, everyone should pay considerable attention to each word, phrase and sentence they are writing.

❑ What happens is the opposite. Most e-mail communication is the equivalent of the writer going to see an internal or external TOP, barking a stream of words at them, many of them mispronounced, and then ending "I trust that is clear," and leaving forthwith.

The two critical causes of these unfortunate outcomes are that:

– We are overloaded with e-mails.
– We are in a rush when answering them.

Looking at each in turn:

We are overloaded with e-mails
One of the biggest nightmares, when returning from a break, is that we know that we are going to be hit with a deluge of e-mails to answer. Some sort of system to process e-mails is vital. Most of you will have a system in place. Ignoring any sub-classifications, I would suggest 4 main classifications:

1. Those you delete straightway.
2. Those that go into "Wait for the first reminder category". You can delete these every three months or so. You rarely get a first reminder, as so many people start off so many hares, which they never pursue.
3. The urgent. These should be subdivided into "ants" (trivial work activities) and "elephants" (activities that are core to job success – that enable you to meet your objectives). Put ants into like groups and eradicate them ASAP. You can use lower standards in order to get rid of them than you would use to catch an elephant. Focus your time on the elephant.
4. The important elephants that are not urgent. These should not be neglected, but looked at regularly and dealt with progressively, so that they do not become stampeding elephants, mingled in with a horde of soldier ants, which have caused the elephants to stampede in the first place and give you nightmares and endless work at weekends, which you never do!

We are in a rush when answering e-mails
Not only do we make silly typos, that irritate the recipient, but we come across as curt and confused! There are many people I know, who are friendly, polite – incredibly good communicators in one-on-one situations. The next moment, I am receiving a reply to an e-mail that

does not mention my name at the beginning or their name at the end. The content is a reply to each of my paragraphs at the end of each paragraph in red.

Some suggested solutions

❑ For elephant e-mails, spend the time it takes to write them properly.

❑ Chapter 5 will enable you to write (and think) with impeccable logic, i.e. communicate in a clear, concise and compelling way.

❑ When pro-active, i.e. initiating the communication, be as friendly as you can. If there is a shared experience, or something important you know has happened to them, then refer to it first – just as you would automatically at a meeting. Try to develop electronic social chit-chat.

There was a PA to an important client I once had. I used a friendly "verbal tone" throughout, introduced some interesting personal experience over a weekend, asked about hers and very soon we had a friendly e-mail rapport. It was extremely helpful, as I made a major mistake with the client. She gave me total support, so that it did not cause any problems in the client relationship.

❑ When it comes to reacting to others' e-mails, then I tend to reflect back both the introduction (or lack of it) and the conclusion (or lack of it) and writing style, though not substance. I do this so that, operating from the subconscious, they think of me as "one of them".

ASK THE RIGHT QUESTION
In this section we cover:

– Use closed questions appropriately.
– Recognise the most effective open questions.
– Top ten tips for success.
– Real-life example of success.

USE CLOSED QUESTIONS APPROPRIATELY

❑ Closed questions require a "Yes" or No" response. They usually begin with an auxiliary verb, e.g. "Do you? Is it? Shall we? Could you? The four effective uses of closed questions are to:

1. Confirm facts, e.g. does 2 and 2 make 4?
2. Acknowledge an emotion, e.g. are you angry with me?
3. Push for a decision, e.g. will you do this piece of work for me?
4. Avoid a conversation, e.g. "Did you have a good weekend?" is much better than saying to a colleague on a Monday morning: "How was your weekend?" TOP might just answer you! With the time-saving closed approach, if the answer is "yes", you can reply "great" and move away, having completed the social nicety in record time.

    If TOP says "no" and it looks as if there is much more to come, you can hastily intervene with "*Sorry to hear that; must dash; catch up with you later to get all the gory details,*" and then off you go – again in record time. "Did you have a good weekend?" is much better than saying, "How was your weekend?"

❏ We have a tendency to use closed questions and avoid open questions – especially as we grow older! This tendency can severely limit the quality of our communication and our ability to have constructive discussion. The four primary reasons for this imbalance are:

1. We are educated into logical thought processes and to find answers.
2. Open questions generate uncertainty as we do not know what the answer will be. This can cause some psychological discomfort especially for controlling types, whose use of closed questions has become habitual in order to get their own way: "Am I right or am I right?" "I have proved my point, have I not?" "Do this, or else."
3. There can be the perception of loss of control of discussions if we don't stick to closed questions. (It is only a perception. The reality is that those who ask probing, open questions control the discussion, as all good interviewers (and negotiators) know as do all those who have been at the receiving end.)
4. Closed questions save time (as in the social example above) and time is very precious to us all.

❑ Because of logical thinking, though life is grey (a mix of black and white), we are all forced to think in black or white. "Guilty or not guilty". "Actually, me Lud, I think I am 23.56% guilty for the following reasons." Take another telling example:

❑ "Were you standing next to the murder victim, whom we have established you hated, with your hands covered in his blood"? "Well, actually..." "Just answer the question put to you – yes or no." "Yes" – 30 years for murder.

❑ "Well, actually, I was going to say that when I came round to have it out with him, I found him with his throat cut. Now I did not like him very much as he had been horrid to me. But I get upset if a little bird dies, never mind a fellow human being. So I tried to stem the flow of blood. Before he died, he looked at me and asked for forgiveness. Of course, I forgave him. He died with a smile on his face." One more "miscarriage of justice".

RECOGNISE THE MOST EFFECTIVE OPEN QUESTIONS

"I kept six honest serving men
They taught me all I knew
Their names were What and Why and When
And How and Where and Who?"
Rudyard Kipling

You cannot answer an open question with a "Yes" or "No". That is why they "open" up a conversation, rather than closing it down. However, their value varies considerably.

WHAT?
"What" is the most versatile open question and has four different functions:

Identifies issues
"What" identifies two types of issue:

Unspecific
❑ What should we talk about?

- ❑ What is the most interesting thing that has happened to you?
- ❑ What did you discuss at the meeting?
- ❑ What did you do yesterday?
- ❑ What have I missed or omitted?
- ❑ What questions should I ask?

Specific

- ❑ What is the problem?
- ❑ What is your vision?
- ❑ What is your objective?
- ❑ What is the decision?

Probes
Gets TOP to think

- ❑ What would be the consequences?
- ❑ What do you mean precisely?
- ❑ What examples can you give?
- ❑ What situations did you face?
- ❑ What kind of people do you employ?
- ❑ What assumptions are you making?

Elicits facts

- ❑ What services do you provide?
- ❑ What are the facts of the matter?
- ❑ What books do you read?

Involves TOP

- ❑ What is your view?
- ❑ What do you think?
- ❑ What decision to you favour?

Can substitute for all the other open questions

❑ What are the reasons for/causes of?	= Why?
❑ What about?	= Why not?
❑ What methods/approaches did you use?	= How?
❑ In what ways is it?	= How?
❑ What are your feelings?	= How do you feel?

❏	What time?	= When?
❏	What place?	= Where
❏	What person?	= Who

WHY?

"Why" has two functions:

Asks for an explanation
Impersonally

❏   Why do we exist?
❏   Why did he do that?
❏   Why did she leave so abruptly?

Personally/critically

❏   Why did you do that?
❏   Why did you make that assumption?
❏   Why did you fail to get authority?

As soon as we ask TOPs to explain their behaviour, it can be taken by them as criticism, especially if accompanied by a harsh tone of voice and hostile body language.

"Critical why" causes untold damage to relationships, because it can cause "blood on the carpet" if both individuals are controlling types. If the individual criticised is a caring type, their fragile self-esteem can be even further reduced, which does not do a lot for their business performance.

So, if necessary, we need to calm ourselves down and communicate in a "cool" way. It is also helpful to reduce the bluntness and brevity of "why" by paraphrasing into a longer introduction:

❏   "It would help me understand the situation better, if you would give me your reasons for doing this?"
❏   "That's an interesting suggestion. Tell me, why do you think it is the best way forward?"
❏   "So, please, tell me the assumptions you made when you did that?"

Determines causes and the causal chain

❑ Why are sales revenues falling?
❑ Why has the quality of our product deteriorated?
❑ Why are we buying in sub-standard raw materials?

HOW?
How has five functions:

Asks for ideas
❑ How can we motivate the bears?
❑ How can we increase morale?

Probes thinking
❑ How do you make a sale?
❑ How do you demonstrate supportive leadership?

Involves
❑ How was your weekend?
❑ How are you feeling?
❑ How would you tackle the problem?

Establishes numerical facts
❑ How old are you?
❑ How often do you hold team meetings?
❑ How many staff report to you?

Establishes price
❑ How much will my pay rise be when I am promoted?

Where, when and who are focused fact-finding questions, i.e. place, time and person.

TOP TEN TIPS FOR SUCCESS
The top ten tips for success as a questioner are:

1. Plan the questions in advance.

2.   Think "open" question.
3.   Use the right wording.
4.   Use perceptive probing questions.
5.   Avoid leading questions.
6.   Avoid loaded questions.
7.   Avoid logical closed alternatives.
8.   Keep questions simple.
9.   Keep questions single.
10. Practise.

1. Plan the questions in advance

Before you attend any important meeting, you should plan the questions in advance – particularly what open questions you need to ask and why. I suggest that the first open question you should ask yourself is:

❑   What is my objective?

The second is:

❑   How will I achieve it?

2. Think open question

❑   The classic of all time, which leads to a very poor relationship between boss and subordinate, is when a closed question is used at the end of a detailed briefing. Assuming it is your boss, he or she will typically finish with something like: "is that all clear?", "do you understand?" You haven't really understood all that much, as it is in an area where your boss is the expert and/or he has been gabbling on non-stop.

❑   However, you say "yes" – don't want to appear stupid. Off you go to do the best you can, work your butt off and present the finished article to your beloved boss. He thinks you knew precisely what was expected of you, and yet you have made, in his eyes, unnecessary mistakes. Worse still, he has to waste his precious time pointing them out to you. You now dislike your boss and he thinks you're incompetent!

❑   If you have a boss, who always asks the closed question, it is in

64

your short-term performance interests (and long-term career interests) to reply along the lines: "Do you mind if I do a quick recap to ensure that I have fully understood your brief and I can do a really good job for you?". (This is long form for the open question, that would be politically incorrect to use: "What did you actually say, boss?") The boss is likely to reply: "Of course not", perhaps adding "but make it quick". (You will be able to make it very quick once you have learnt how to think and write with impeccable logic – see Chapter 5).

❑ This leads to another helpful hint. Note down key points, when being given a brief. Research was carried out amongst university students on how much they could remember after a presentation, depending on what they did. Each group was asked to carry out a different activity, i.e:

1. Concentrate on listening.
2. Take copious notes, writing down as much as they could.
3. Concentrate on listening, but this group were also told that they would be given hand-outs at the end.
4. Focus on writing down the key points only.

The order of maximum memory retention was 4 by far, followed by 2, with 1 a distant third, and 3 in fourth place.

❑ Another example is, when we have finished summarising what TOP has said, we then ask the closed question: "am I right?", to which we tend to get the reply "Yes", especially if we are in a more senior position. A far better approach is to conclude with the open question: "What have I omitted?" This explicitly acknowledges that we are, in fact, human and can make mistakes and enables a reply: "Well, actually, I did mention that I had resigned from the company."

❑ A final example is that, when we open up with "let us establish the facts of the matter", we should not conclude with "so that's agreed" but probe further with "and let us think of any information we may have overlooked," before closing down to move to the next stage in the conversation.

3. Use the right wording

❑　If you say to TOP: "*What do you mean?*" TOP might just say: "I mean what I say." If you add the word "precisely", it focuses TOP and TOP is very unlikely to say: "*I mean what I say precisely*" (and certainly not if under the influence of alcohol).

❑　If you say to TOP or a group of TOPs: "*What are all the possible suggestions we can have to solve this problem?*" that wording will produce far, far, more ideas than the bald: "*How do we solve this problem?*"

❑　Similarly: "*What do you think are all the possible reasons why our relationship is bad at the moment?*" will produce a greater range of causes than just: "*Why do you think our relationship is bad at the moment?*"

4. Use perceptive probing questions

❑　A perceptive probing question is one that you can only ask, when you have become a good listener. [See the section on listening in this chapter.]

❑　When you ask good open questions, the other person opens up. That is their purpose. When they are in a relaxed state and in full flow, they almost invariably drop in a phrase or even a sentence that is significant. This is inevitable, as you are getting them to think – to reveal what was hidden from you or to reveal what was latent or subconscious (hidden from them) and/or come up with completely new thoughts.

❑　If you are listening acutely, you can easily pick up this phrase, as there will be a slight change in tone of voice and body language. Often the revealing phrase will be prefaced by the word "actually". Once you have listened, then you pounce: "So you mentioned that you had a few difficulties with the client". "So what precisely were those difficulties?" said in a caring, empathetic way, of course.

5. Avoid leading questions
Leading questions can be phrased in a closed or open style, and are the

antithesis to promoting discovery or even problem-solving, as they push or lead to the "one right answer".

❑ "The chairman thinks we should sack Jones. What do you think?"
❑ "Surely you do not have any doubts about our new mission?"

6. Avoid loaded questions

With a leading question, our own views are implicit. In a loaded question, they are explicit or loaded in.

❑ "Do you not agree that John has poor time-keeping?"
❑ "Why don't you drop dead!?"

Not a very open question!

7. Avoid "logical" closed alternatives

❑ Let us say that the issue under discussion is "a drop in sales". "Well clearly we have to either reduce costs or increase revenues. Which do you favour?" Far, far better to go the open route: "Let us consider all the options we could take to reverse this trend" or even better: "Let us think of all the possible causes of this problem."

❑ After all, for all we know, the root cause could be demotivation of staff (which might come out of pursuing the options route) or the first signs of a market moving into decline, which may require a new strategy, like diversification, which might come from taking the causal route.

❑ Incidentally, "or" can be used exclusively, as in the above case, or conjunctively, i.e. both alternatives can be selected. Both types should be avoided.

8. Keep questions simple

❑ On a video we have a persuasion role-play between two managers, where one took more than ten minutes to ask his question. You should have seen the body language of the listener!

❏   If we are not confident, or we are too involved, or we are too rushed and speak before we think, we can get lost. We can start a question, go on a gentle ramble or lecture tour, recover, and revert back to the question in hand.

❏   This is to be avoided, as it makes us look silly, and puts the listener to sleep! We must keep our questions simple and to the point.

9. Keep questions single

❏   A golden rule of effective questioning is "one at a time". More than one question can lead to confusion or evasion. The respondent can select which one to answer, and the other one or ones can be lost in the subsequent discussion.

❏   A classic example of this (and to avoid logical closed alternatives) occurred in the UK when the Conservative Party was in Government in the 1990s. A backbench Labour MP put forward written questions, intended to embarrass the government by showing the extent of sex discrimination in the Civil Service. Not only did he ask multiple questions, but ended by asking whether male staff or female staff were in the majority!

❏   The junior minister's written reply to the entire set of questions was one word – yes!

10. Practise

❏   Many readers will have developed a closed question mindset for the reasons given earlier in this chapter. So you will need to create a new habit, which you now know how to do.

❏   I have run numerous sessions where one manager is the Questioner and Listener (Q&L) and the other is the client or problem holder (PH). The job of the Q&L is to help the PH define the problem successfully and then help PH find their own solution. The other managers are there to take notes and provide feedback.

❏   On one occasion, Q&L asked his client one open question: "What is your problem?" He (Q&L was a male) then proceeded to ask 14 closed questions. He ended up pushing the wrong solution to the wrong problem to an extremely irritated client.

❑ Almost all Q&Ls will start with an open question, and then proceed to answer it themselves and finish up either pushing the one right answer or logically closed alternatives onto their client.

❑ The only Q&Ls to get it right first time have been women. They have got it right by only asking open questions or with the vast majority open, with one or two of the "appropriate" closed questions.

❑ So if you want to become an effective questioner, you need to discipline yourself to only ask open questions, with the very occasional appropriately used closed question. Once successful, repeat success 20 times until it has become a habit. Then you will be the best Q&L in your organisation, exceed your business development targets, have successful business relationships and (taking account all the other helpful hints contained in this book) be well on the way to taking the fast track to the top.

❑ We conclude this section with a case study of success, entitled:"Promoting Discovery"

Promoting discovery

Jane: "So what's the problem, Brian?"

Brian: "Well, Jane, it's like this. I am in charge of four teams, each with a team-leader, and one of my team-leaders has resigned. So I have to choose, as I see it, between recruiting a new team-leader, promoting from the team without replacement, or promoting from within and recruiting a new team-member. I have complete autonomy as to the decision I make."

Jane: "That's interesting. It's rare these days to have complete autonomy. What did your boss advise?"

[Using the open "what" enables the questioner to proffer advice by way of assumption that won't cause offence. It is sensible with major decisions to seek the advice/support of your boss. If, not likely in this case, Brian had not, then the open question suggests he should in a non-controversial way. So, if advice had not been sought, the conversation might proceed:

Promoting discovery

Brian: *"Well, actually, I haven't talked to my boss about this. Do you think I should?"*

Jane: *"Well, I think it is a good idea with important decisions to talk to your boss, so that you can find out what her views are. If she agrees with you, at least she is in the know and will support you. What do you think?"*

This is much better than a closed approach:

Jane: *"Have you talked to your boss?"*

Brian: *"No."*

Jane: *"Well, don't you think you should?"*

Brian: "Well, reading between the lines, I think that she would like me to go the route of minimum expenditure – promote from the team and don't replace. To be fair to her, she did say that, if I thought it necessary, she would support recruitment."

Jane: "So – if you do decide to recruit, you will have to make a good case."

Brian: "Absolutely."

Pause

Jane: "Well, before we consider the pros and cons of each option, tell me what other changes are taking place which could impact on your decision."

[Probing, and assuming, as is almost inevitable in a world of change, that there will be a bigger picture to the problem than initially provided. This question unlocks the real problem. If it is answered in the negative, no harm is done. If the core issue is confirmed as the original problem, the conversation can proceed to solutions and actions.]

Brian: "Funny you should ask that – but there are a couple of changes that muddy the water. First of all, I am taking on a bigger job, and secondly I am on the move."

Jane: "I see. Looking at the job first, in what ways will it be bigger?"

Promoting discovery

Brian: "Well, I am taking on a new team in addition to my existing team. This team is situated 50 miles from where I work now."

Jane: "And that is where you are moving?" [*Closed to confirm the facts.*]

Brian "Yes – in 3 months."

Jane: "I see – and what do you think will be the impact on your existing teams?"

Brian: "Well – all the problems of managing at a distance. We have an excellent team-spirit amongst the team-leaders and myself, and that will take a nose-dive, because we won't see so much of each other, and it will be much more difficult for me to stay in touch with developments, help solve problems and so on."

Jane: "Let's pause for a moment and see if I understand the situation. The core issue is how to keep your team-leaders motivated and the teams effective, given that you will be physically absent and have to allocate chunks of time to handle your additional team responsibilities. What have I missed out?" [*Summarizing and using an open question to ensure points Jane might have missed are mentioned by Brian.*]

Brian: "Well, nothing really, as the replacement issue is part of the overall problem we have agreed."

Jane: "Good. So how can we solve the problem – what do you think you can do about it?"

Brian: "Well, that's a tricky one. One thing's for sure: I will have to recruit a new team-leader. None of the existing team are ready for promotion, nor is the timing right, it would not be on to leave one team short-staffed, with the problems the teams face with my departure. I need all the resources I can get. But what else to do, I don't know. Have you any ideas, Jane?"

[*Interesting, when the core issue is the "bigger picture"- the more strategic issue – then the original problem can quickly be solved. Vision provides focus for action. Additionally, when asked for advice, because TOP has run out of ideas, then provide it. You do not become an open questioning robot.*]

Promoting discovery

Jane: "Well, I think so. What about an on-site co-coordinator?"

Brian: "What do you mean precisely?"

Jane: "Well, have one of your team-leaders take on the role of co-co-ordinator of the teams, when you are not there – and report regularly to you between the meetings."

Brian: "Yes – that's an interesting proposition – but what about putting the noses of the other team-leaders out of joint?" Pause. "I think I have it – rotate the role amongst all the team-leaders, so each has it for 3 months of the year. I think we've cracked it?"

Jane: "So, what do you need to do?" [*Now the problem has been resolved, moving to action.*]

Brian: "Well, get onto Personnel straightaway, so that we start the recruitment process. With a bit of luck, we can get a good internal candidate in place within 3 months. Then tell my team-leaders of my new role, and what I propose to do both on the co-coordinating front and the replacement front – and get some feedback."

Jane: "And what should you do first of all, putting a political hat on?" [*A little bit of gentle steering.*]

Brian: "Ah! Yes – early meeting with the boss to get her agreement and make the case for the replacement, then onto Personnel and then the team-meeting."

Jane: "And when do you think you can do these?"

Brian: "No problem. I will talk to my boss tomorrow morning, telephone Personnel in the afternoon and tell my team-members at the regular meeting next Monday."

Jane: "Good. So how do you feel about things now?"

Brian: "A damn sight better than before we had this chat. Thanks a lot for all your help, Jane – much appreciated."

KEY POINTS

❑ The sequence of questions was What? What? What? How?

Where? What? What? (these uncovered the core issue) How? (phrased using: In what ways?), Closed to confirm facts, Why not? (phrased using: What about?), What?, When?, and an "involving" How? to finish.

❑ Effective conversations always have a discovery element, due to the quality of the questioning and listening skills of at least one party. Through Jane's gentle probing, as well as helpful advice, both parties contributed to the positive outcome, which was discovered during the conversation.

LISTEN EFFECTIVELY

In this section we look at:

❑ The importance of listening.
❑ How to be effective.

IMPORTANCE OF LISTENING

❑ Have you ever been in a situation (and I would be very surprised if you had not) when you were talking and the person you were talking to clearly was not listening to a word you said? Can you recall, looking back, how you felt about this?

❑ To develop an understanding of the importance of listening, managers are put into pairs. One is briefed to talk for 2 minutes on something they are passionate about and the other to do everything in their power, bar walking from the room, to indicate lack of listening, e.g. avoiding eye contact/watching someone else, fidgeting.

❑ When we debrief the exercise, we ask the talking manager how poor listening affected them, both in terms of emotions felt and actions taken. A typical set of answers is:

– I was angry and annoyed with the listener (one manager used the word "hated").
– The listener showed complete lack of respect.
– I lost concentration.
– I felt a fool.

- I found that I was repeating what I had said previously.
- I felt confidence and self-esteem drain away.

❏ Poor listening, especially if it has become a habit, is the single greatest way to destroy the relationship with TOP. Conversely, listening effectively to TOP is the single greatest way to build the relationship. In the bible, it says: "It is better to give than to receive". To develop good relationships with any TOP, it is better to listen than to talk.

❏ As David Butler, our outdoor development guru, used to say to the managers/executives: "God gave us two ears and one mouth for a reason". He is a quietly spoken man, but he always had his audience's undivided attention – no doubt due to the fact that there is always a certain amount of fear and trepidation when facing the unknown in an outdoor environment!

❏ When we listen, we show interest, and everyone warms to anyone who shows interest in them. More importantly, we say, without using a single word: *"I think you are an important human being, whose opinions and thoughts I value"*. We give them respect; we build up their confidence and self-esteem. They will reciprocate, and we will have started on the virtuous path to an effective relationship.

HOW TO BE EFFECTIVE

There are eight ways to becoming effective listeners. These are to:

1. Be committed.
2. Be objective.
3. Suspend judgement.
4. Check for understanding.
5. Use positive body language.
6. Use words.
7. Ask follow-up questions.
8. Appreciate silence.

1. Be committed

❏ We need to recognise and believe in the power of effective listening – that, unless we listen effectively, we have wasted all those good open questions. We have to want to listen "actively". "Actively" is an excellent word, because it conveys the reality that we have to consciously act to listen.

2. Be objective

❑ We need to think, make that deliberate pause, and take that deep breath. It is our feelings, our opinions, our prejudices (whether against TOP or the content) or our nerves which deny us effective listening.

❑ The effective listener learns how to take control, not of others, but of themselves. Taking the time out, as a discussion starts, to say to ourselves *"I am going to listen"* will improve our skill. Deliberately pausing, when that comment comes which will trigger an instant negative logical or emotional response, will improve our skill. In short, being proactive, not reactive.

❑ Only when we have listened to ourselves can we listen effectively to TOP.

3. Suspend judgment

If we judge before TOP speaks, we don't really listen. If we judge in the act of listening, there are two outcomes:

We disagree

❑ If we don't want to express our disagreement, we will be turned off and lapse into passive listening, thus denying an effective conversation. This passive listening can lead to the outcome, (which annoys so many TOPs because they don't understand the reason), where we verbally commit to doing things we don't believe in or want to do, and so either do badly or not at all, if we can find a good excuse later!

❑ If we want to express our disagreement, we will move into "listening interruptus", where we do not hear a word TOP says and are waiting to seize the speaking crown.

❑ The subsequent flow from us of point making and closed questions will deny an effective conversation. This will lead to a quarrel if TOP responds aggressively to our aggression, the likely response from a controlling type. It will lead to verbal acceptance only, the likely response from a caring type.

We agree

❑ That may seem fine, but early agreement will lose some little nuances or new angles that are lost because we have stopped listening.

4. Check for understanding

How often do both parties assume understanding, only to be rudely awakened subsequently by actions inconsistent with the understanding assumed? So:

❑ Pause to recap – summarize the key points TOP has made.

❑ Get agreement from TOP before moving on – confirm your understanding is complete with an open question (as demonstrated in the example of effective questioning.)

5. Use positive body language

❑ As we already know, the words we speak have only 7% per cent of the total impact in face-to-face communication. The way we speak – the tones, modulation, intensity, phrasing and use of pauses – has 38% per cent of total impact, and our body language – our gestures, posture and facial expression – a highly significant 55 per cent.

❑ If we are listening effectively, then we will display the right body language. If we consciously try to use the right body language, we will probably feel awkward, but we will be better listeners, just as those who smiled down the phone became better salespeople. So let us consider facial expression, gestures and body posture:

Facial expression

❑ Facial expressions should reflect the feelings being expressed. If TOP is feeling sad, look sad, if happy, look happy, and if angry, look angry – angry together at the source of TOP's anger.

❑ If you are the source of anger, that's a different kettle of fish. Then, you take a *cool pause* and move into *reflective listening* (see next section). A *cool pause* consists of taking a deep breath, holding it in for as long as you can, slowly exhaling and holding it out for as long as possible. It literally "clears your head". Practice will enable you to do this without the TOP being aware – only that you are pausing, which enables TOP to calm down a little.

❑ If there are no emotions being expressed, as TOP is in logical mode, then look confident and thoughtful. You are in the rational adult ego state or "cool mode" together.

❑ There should be fairly frequent eye contact, but never a glare or stare. Such eye contact stops you becoming distracted and conveys the message that you are, in fact, all ears.

❑ It is quite helpful to ask for (and invariably be given) permission to take notes. You can then look down to make a note, rather than sideways, over the TOP's shoulder or down to the floor.

Gestures

❑ Gestures are for the speaking TOP and not the listener. Through using appropriate gestures, the impact of TOP's message is significantly enhanced. Gestures from the listener act as a distraction – a form of non-verbal interruption.

Posture

❑ There is not a single right posture, as the posture will vary according to the situation – the logic or emotion being expressed, the ebb and flow of the conversation. However, in all situations, a "cool" posture should be adopted, not an aggressive nor submissive one.

❑ For instance, when seated, the listener could take up an open position (neither legs nor arms folded), lean forward slightly, with the head a little to one side, and hands clasped loosely together, resting on the lap.

❑ There are variations such as leaning back slightly to accommodate the other person leaning forward; open posture, with one hand on the chin and the other supporting the elbow or sitting straight with legs slightly apart, each hand resting on the appropriate knee. This last position is the best position for the back, and is known as the Pharaoh's posture.

❑ Another technique you can use to help the development of empathy as regards both posture and action is *reflection* or *mirroring*. You will have all experienced this. I recall vividly that, at one of the many hundreds of course dinners I have hosted, four of us around the corner of the dining room table got into a long, thoughtful and enlightening conversation. I noticed, at the time, that we were all leaning forward with our elbows on the table throughout, and whenever one picked up their glass to drink some wine, we all did.

❑ So observe the body language of the speaking TOP and mirror it. You are operating powerfully on TOP's subconscious. The TOP literally sees "one of us".

6. Use words

An effective listener uses words in the right tone to convey the right meaning. There are two aspects – reflection and interest:

Reflection

We reflect back the end of an interesting sentence, e.g. "You fell off your bike, did you?" or, to mix it up, paraphrase and expand, e.g. "That fall must have been a nasty experience for you."

Interest

Show interest by those little verbal noises or even words. The murmur "mmmmhuh" (or variations, which I will not try to spell) or "Well, I never", "You don't say" or simply "I agree". "I agree" is always music to TOP's ears.

7. Ask follow-up open questions

The focus should be the "promoting discovery" what, why or how. For example:

❑ "So why do you think he was so rude to you?"
❑ "How on earth did you get out of that predicament?"

❑ "Good heavens, so what happened next?"

8. Appreciate silence

❑ We tend to dislike silence, and rush in verbally to fill it. A natural discomfort with silence may often impair our active listening, either because we do not pause to collect our thoughts and give a measured response – ask the right question – or we speak when it would have better from TOP's point of view if we had remained silent.

❑ We can, by being silent, give TOP time to control emotions or gather thoughts, or simply share together a pleasant mood or ambience.

❑ As Mozart said: *"Silence is the profoundest sound in music"*.

Author's notes

❑ When you have finished listening, you have two choices:

1. Use the relevant open probing question to enable the speaker to continue speaking and you continue listening.
2. Used closed questions to close off the speaker. You can then stop the conversation or make any points you want to make.

❑ You can always tell if a TOP is lying, as the TOP cannot control his or her reaction, which is driven from the subconscious.

❑ When we are young children, our subconscious tries to create a pre-lie situation, as soon as we are caught out. So we put our hands to our mouths to shove the lie back from whence it came. This is unsuccessful.

❑ As we grow older, we become more skilled in controlling this "tell". As adults, we limit our tells to a small cluster of involuntary movements i.e. looking down to avoid eye contact as well as brushing the top of our lips with a forefinger.

❑ People who need to be skilled liars e.g. politicians and poker players, train themselves to eradicate these tells. They can look you directly in the eye, and then lie. What most of them don't know is that, if challenged, the eyes still reveal the lie. Involuntarily, there is a slight contraction of the pupil- the sophisticated equivalent of shoving the lie back down your throat. Hence the wearing of shades in poker to avoid one expert being able to "read" another expert's bluff.

REFLECTIVE LISTENING

❑ This is an extraordinary powerful and effective technique. Whenever TOP is aggressive towards you for some perceived mistake you have made, use it. It is just as effective, whether the aggression occurs over the phone or face-to-face.

❑ Let us take an example. Your boss, John, dashes into your office and barks aggressively: "The deadline for your project paper was 12 noon. It is now 2 pm and I need it right away".

❑ John's communication contained a fact – that you had missed the agreed deadline; a need – that he had to have your project paper right and an emotion – anger towards you. Incidentally, all communications contain, at most, these three components.

❑ What we usually do, in reply, is to acknowledge our mistake (their fact), apologise for it, try to explain it away and then promise to correct it ASAP - meet their need. That approach generates a perception of incompetence in your boss's eyes. "Reflective listening" reverses this perception. You need to take three actions:

1. Stay "cool".
2. Eliminate TOP's emotion.
3. Meet the need.

Looking at each in turn:

1. Stay "cool"

❑ To avoid slipping into either aggression or passivity, when faced by an irrational emotional controller, you must maintain the "cool" state that will become your norm in the work-place.

❑ To do so, straightaway deploy the "cool pause" or pauses.

2. Eliminate TOP's emotion

❑   Until you can return TOP back into a rational adult state, TOP will continue to be an irrational controller. So you have to address and only address the emotion first (and sometimes second, third, fourth and so on) until the aggressor has calmed down and returned to adulthood. Then and only then do you address the need.

❑   Even when people have recognised the need to address the emotional state first, unwittingly, they often add fuel to the flames, e.g. "I can see you are a little upset, John". To which comes the reply: "I am not a little upset, as you put it, Kate, I am very angry." The secret is never to understate the degree of emotion, but deliberately overstate it. "I can see that you are really furious with me, John, and I am sorry to have caused it" (or words to that effect). "I am not furious – just a bit annoyed," comes the reply.

❑   There is a subtle psychological process at play. When individuals are aggressive, they simply want you to do what they want done straightaway. They are itching to have a fight with you, and will be subconsciously driven to disagree with anything you say. When you understate the emotional intensity, they have to disagree and say: "I am very angry." Now, if somebody says out loud they are very angry, the need for street cred and the power of auto-suggestion means they must become very angry. You pour fuel on the flames, and get severely burnt as a result.

❑   The converse, therefore, holds true. They automatically disagree with your statement that they are very furious, counter with the statement: "I am, actually, only a little bit annoyed". Then they start becoming only a little bit annoyed. This process is helped by the fact that, again subconsciously, they want to avoid the wrong label. Lots of bosses don't mind having a reputation of being a firm, authoritative leader. Few want the label of "Mr. or Mrs. Furious" in the company!

3. Meet the need

Once John is back to normal, you conclude with: "The final version of the paper will be on your desk by 3 pm."

Key points

❑ A key benefit of reflective listening is that, at no point, do you either acknowledge or apologise for the "mistake" (only for causing the emotion), and so you do not have to justify it. You leave TOP (in this case, your boss) with the memory of competence rather incompetence. If you had apologised for the mistake, you have admitted it and bosses, typically, don't like listening to a load of excuses or "whining". If you go the non-reflective listening route, you just confirm your incompetence in their eyes.

❑ Moreover, there always two sides to any "mistake". It may well be a "fact" for John that you have missed the deadline, i.e. made a mistake. However, there are "facts" for you, e.g. John endlessly dumps work on you, never provides proper briefings, and his deadlines are rather elastic – the work just sits on his desk day after day, i.e. three mistakes in your eyes. No, a great idea to use "reflective listening" to avoid heated discussion of "mistakes" and the reduction in quality of a relationship that is key to your career success.

❑ The reason why the technique is called "reflective listening" is because you listen to the emotion and reflect (and exaggerate) that back before addressing the need, and ignoring the "fact".

NEGOTIATING OUTCOMES THAT ARE SUCCESSFUL FOR BOTH PARTIES – WIN/WINS

We, consciously or subconsciously, are regularly negotiating with all our key TOPs. Research was carried out into what made negotiators, who had a track record of outstanding success, so effective. Set out below are all the strategies they adopted:

ACTIVELY SEEK AND AGREE COMMON GROUND FIRST

❑ This can be a shared goal, value or principle. The devil is in the detail. If you start with detail items first, you will guarantee failure. Detail should be avoided until common ground is established. Generate a win/win early on as it creates trust and rapport. It ensures that the later, more detailed, discussions are much more likely to succeed.

❑ In short, if you agree first, then any disagreements will be easily resolved. If you disagree first, you will never reach agreement.

DEMONSTRATE RESPECT

❑ Seek to understand, as much as to be understood. The skilled negotiator spends 20% of the time asking (open) questions, while the average negotiator only 10%. Questions give control over the discussion, and are a more acceptable alternative to direct disagreement. They give negotiators breathing space to marshal their thoughts – and demonstrate respect.

TEST UNDERSTANDING AND SUMMARISE

❑ Skilled negotiators are concerned to ensure clarity. They spend twice as much time as average negotiators testing understanding and summarising the stage negotiations have reached. Their focus is on ensuring that any agreement will be successfully implemented.

❑ Average negotiators will often display over-anxiety to reach an agreement. They will often fail to test understanding for fear that making things explicit could lead to further disagreement. Such an approach gives rise to problems when implementing an agreement and inspires mistrust.

BE OPEN, AND NOT DEFENSIVE, IN STATING PLANS, INTENTIONS AND MOTIVATIONS
This is self-explanatory.

MAKE CONCESSIONS AS TRADE-OFFS

❑ For example: "I will give you this if you will give me that. What do you think?" If you don't give anything, the process is doomed to fail, unless you have sufficient power to force your position through in its entirety. That would appear to be a "win" for you and a "lose" for TOP. However, TOP will nurse a grudge, will get back at you as soon as an opportunity arises in the future and your relationship will go down the pan.

❑ If, on the other hand, you just give in to TOP on one of their points, TOP will perceive you as weak and make sure you give in again and again.

AVOID NEGATIVITY AND DISPLAY FEELINGS DELIBERATELY
i.e. under control and in moderation – be "cool".

ADOPT TOP'S TERMINOLOGY AND VIEWPOINT WHERE IT DOES NOT UNDERMINE YOUR OWN POSITION OR THE JOINT GOAL
We have already made this point in the second chapter. We will develop it in Chapter 6, "Succeed in the Political World".

SIGNAL A PARTICULAR BEHAVIOUR IN ADVANCE

❑ Successful negotiators are 5 times more likely to give an indication of the type of behaviour they are about to use. Instead of just asking: "How will that affect the bottom line?" they say: "May I ask a question at this juncture?" This catches TOP's attention, and alerts TOP to the fact that there is a question in the offing. When TOP gives you permission along the lines of "of course, you may," you then ask your question.

❑ Additionally, it slows down the pace of interchange, provides a pause and reduces any element of cut and thrust that has occurred. Similarly, if you have a proposal to make or idea to put forward, you would say to TOP: "May I make a suggestion?" and then make it, after TOP has agreed.

Author's notes

❑ Whenever you ask anyone to do anything suddenly, (and so from their perspective unexpectedly), you will get a negative response – initially. The reaction or transition curve and effective change

❏ management generally are covered in Chapter 9, "Create Growth from Change".

❏ Hence the use, when trying to close a verbose TOP down, of the question: "May I please interrupt?"

AVOID IRRITANTS

❏ Most negotiators have the sense not to make unfavourable comments about the other side. However, average negotiators are more likely to say gratuitously favourable things about themselves, using expressions such as "fair", "reasonable". Skilled negotiators avoid such value loaded expressions as they irritate TOP by implying that TOP is being "unfair" or "unreasonable".

AVOID ATTACK /DEFENCE SPIRALS

❏ Average negotiators often become heated and then use value-loaded epithets or expressions that belittle TOP. This behaviour tends to form a spiral of increasing intensity. One negotiator will attack. TOP will defend, usually in a manner that the first negotiator sees as an attack. So the first attacks TOP more forcefully and a vicious spiral to "irretrievable breakdown" begins. The study showed that average negotiators use more than 3 times as much attacking/defending behaviour as skilled negotiators.

REDUCE/AVOID COUNTER-PROPOSALS

❏ Negotiations can resemble table-tennis matches – a proposal put by one party is immediately met by a counter-proposal. Such tactics cloud the clarity of negotiations, and are seen by TOP as blocking tactics. Skilled negotiators use fewer counterproposals.

FOCUS ON KEY REASONS

❏ One of the surprising differences between skilled and average negotiators is that the skilled ones use fewer reasons to back up their arguments. Most of us believe that the more arguments we use, the more likely we are to tip the balance our way. In reality, if more arguments are advanced, more points are available for dispute. If the negotiator gives 5 reasons, and the third is weak, TOP will concentrate on that.

Author's note
As a very skilled negotiator, taking in points already made in the book, you should beat the surveyed skilled negotiators by:

1. The vast majority of your questions being open and only using the appropriate closed questions.
2. Being the "coolest kid on the block".
3. Having no attack/defence spirals as you never attack and know how to respond to an attack from TOP.
4. Harnessing the power of SPO. This was, necessarily, not part of the original research findings. It is very effective indeed. So repeat as often as possible and emphasise slightly, when repeating, any core message that you want to get home. Eventually the TOP's subconscious will tell the conscious self that it is an irrefutable fact.

Chapter 4

Develop Competence in Non-Preferred Areas

INTRODUCTION

❏   We start this chapter by looking at the need to value diversity and then consider practical proven strategies that enable you to become more complete – more confident and confident in any area that is not naturally preferred, and where you would like to focus.

❏   Specifically we look at how any individual can:

- Become more extroverted
- Develop the introvert
- Develop their caring side
- Develop their controlling side
- Become more logical and practical
- Improve creativity
- Improve flexible and planning skills

VALUING DIFFERENCE

❏   As we know, natural opposites dislike each other. This can be summed up in the first (new version) of the Jack Spratt nursery rhyme, where Jack and Jackie Spratt were opposites on the fat/lean dimension.

"Jack Spratt could eat no fat, Jackie could eat no lean
No problemo as together they had never been."

❑ Typically, there are rarely complete opposites in preferences and, typically, each party makes some effort to understand and live with the differences. So we have compromise – recognition of the difference and acceptance – finding a workable solution.

❑ Now the Spratt's favourite dish they shared together was roast pork. In their world of compromise, Jack would religiously scrape off all the fat. He would then cook the pork and eat the rather dry and tasteless end product, but he knew no better. Jackie, on receiving the fat from Jack, would remove every single trace of lean, and then cook it and eat it – a rather bland and samey taste, but she knew no better.

> *"Jack Spratt could eat no fat, Jackie could eat no lean;*
> *Yet betwixt the two of them, they licked the platter clean".*

❑ Over time they can create completeness within themselves and with each other in the dimensions, where difference exists. This requires a fundamental shift in attitude towards the non-preferred side.

❑ What we have to do is follow the advice of Carl Jung, who wrote in 1933; "*A typology is designed, first and foremost, as an aid to a psychological critique of knowledge…...The valuable thing here is the critical attempt to prevent oneself from taking one's own prejudices as the criterion for normality.*"

❑ I prefer to put it in a more favourable light. The first step to individual completeness is to recognise that what we perceive as the dark or "wild" side of each dimension is, in fact, lit up by the soft brilliance of a full moon on a cold, frosty, sparkling winter's night. We then can learn to "walk on the wild side".

Walk on the wild side

Let us now assume that both Jackie and Jack had recognised the "moonlight" – that difference could potentially add value, that a key to personal growth is experimentation, trying different things out. Because of this belief, they respected each other and said to each other. "If you like fat/lean – then maybe it is not all bad".

They then took the first step towards a fundamental change – a little risk, but entirely consistent with their current liking of fat/lean. They cooked the pork in its own natural juices and produced some fantastic crackling and meat, enriched with its own juices.

They separated out the fat and lean and Jack started tucking into his lean and Jackie into her fat. First of all Jack exclaimed: "This is the best bit of lean, I have ever, ever tasted", met almost simultaneously by Jackie's shriek of delight: "This is the best bit of fat I have ever, ever, tasted"

In fact, they did more and each, very tentatively, tasted the other's delight and found it was not quite as bad as they had been lead to believe (as the hated lean had traces of that lovely fat and the hated fat had traces of that lovely lean).

Instead of compromise, over time, they would achieve a real Win/Win where added value had been produced, both in terms of their own personal growth and the growth of the relationship between them.

"Jack and Jackie Spratt loved both fat and lean
And every day together they licked the platter clean."

BECOMING MORE EXTROVERTED

We start by revisiting the case study "proving" Iceberg's First Law: "Every stimulus produces a response" or "First impressions count."

The wrong approach

Let us take an example. Introverts with a client-facing role can find themselves in what, for them, are quite nerve-wracking situations. An example would be when they are under a three line whip to attend a networking event with clients or prospects. They have to join a group of stranger TOPs.

What they fail to appreciate is that one or more members of the group notice them before they speak, either in the act of joining or well before. What they also fail to realise is that their body language as they approach, driven by their fears and worries, conveys precisely that the last place they want to be is where they are and the last thing they want to do is what they are about to do.

This stimulus, driven from the subconscious, produces a negative response from the group of TOPs – again driven from their subconscious. Their reception meets their worst fears. This compounds the problem for the future. It also drives deeper their feelings of inadequacy and low self-esteem. They then start finding all the excuses they can to avoid such painful events in the future.

This means that they do not meet their business development targets. This is a highly career regressive move. It has a negative impact on their performance, image and relationship with their boss.

❑ Now to the solution, provided to me by an introvert on a development programme, who was the top performer when it came to business development.

❑ First of all you have to practice at approaching the group in a "cool" way, before attending the event.

❑ When you get there, you look for an odd-numbered group (say, to start with, 3, 5 or 7). Now the nature of group dynamics is that, after introductions and any posturing/superb performances from the practised extroverts, dominating the conversation and so on, the group, whilst physically still together, breaks down into a series of 1-1 conversations. So there will be one individual, who is on their own and isolated. Wait, patience is a virtue, until you espy such an individual. Then, confidently, you go up and introduce yourself to the TOP. So you have joined a group by meeting an individual.

❏ Introverts tend to be good at developing one-on-one relationships. So they are playing to their natural strengths and staying within their comfort zone. There are two reasons why the introverted guy, who told me this, outperformed all the extroverts.

1. Extroverts tend to meet many people but not focus on one. By developing a one-on-one, he was able to develop the relationship much further than the extroverts, and almost always arrange for another meeting and get it firmly into diaries.

2. Initially, the first target TOP could be anyone from the client or prospects. It would be a small client and a junior member of that client or prospect team. As his confidence grew, he would work out who was the big client fish and who was the key player. As soon as that player was on their own or the odd person out in group, he would move in for the profitable kill.

❏ A final point is that, as your confidence grows and you become more and more successful in the group environment, you become much more prepared to move out of your expanded comfort zone – and actually join an even-number group. Eventually you become not bad at all in group settings and, if you had an original score of 3 in extroversion, this will have changed, over time, to a 2.

DEVELOPING THE INTROVERT

❏ Plan (if you are an Organiser) or make a spur of the moment decision (if you are a Flexible) to whisk yourself off to the countryside early one Sunday morning, providing you have abstained from alcohol the previous evening. Go for a long leisurely walk on your own in the morning. Have a relaxed pub lunch. Set yourself the goal of making a connection with someone in the pub and find out everything you can about him or her – develop empathy with a random TOP. Then write up a full report on the TOP.

❏ If that seems a step too far for you at the moment, then simply start going for walks on your own in the country and build up to the final exercise. You see many extroverts, if not most, as I pointed out in Chapter 2, do not recognise that introversion exists either externally (TOPs who are introverted) or within themselves.

Author's notes

❏ There is a Yin/Yang in this dimension and the control/care dimension. A well known phenomenon in the celebrity world is socialites going into excess in extroversion. Eventually, excess in Extroverted Yin produces a sudden switch into Introverted Yang – the drying out clinic. [If excessively extroverted people commit a crime and are sent to prison, they go "stir crazy", as they cannot handle an excessively introverted environment for any length of time.]

❏ Caring women (and it can be caring men, of course) when verbally and physically abused by excessively controlling male partners/spouses (and it can be excessively controlling women, of course) turn into worms – doormats that blame themselves, and whose confidence and self-esteem are shattered. They go into excess care mode and can stay there for long periods of time.

❏ Eventually, the excess in Caring Yin (action and reaction are equal and opposite) produces a sudden switch into excess Controlling Yang and the now instantly hated object (her former beloved) is dispatched with whatever weapon comes to hand. Incidentally, the excess Controlling Yang is Mr Hyde. When he disappears, the woman "comes to" and tells the truth to the Police. "*I suddenly snapped. I don't know what came over me. It was as if I was a completely different person*".

❏ What happens is that many extroverts simply don't like their own company. They only spend time with themselves because they have to – to complete tasks that they have to do on their own. I have noticed that a number of extroverts, who have given a score of 2 to introversion, have been brought up in natural countryside environments.

❑ Once you have started to look forward to your walks with nature, then you can go for the more complete introverted project.

❑ You need to carry out effective introverted behaviour successfully (i.e. with enjoyment) at least 21 times for you to become complete – comfortable and confident in displaying introverted behaviour. This means, and this holds for the other non-preferred areas, that you will be able to connect with other introverts and with your own introverted side, whenever you so consciously choose.

❑ By achieving completeness, you take conscious control.

CONTROLLING EFFECTIVELY

We have already covered this in the previous chapter. Whether you are naturally a controlling type of person or a naturally a caring type of person, if you can learn to develop "cool" behaviour more and more in your working (and non-working) life, you will be operating in what is termed the rational adult ego state, where you are in conscious control of your communication and have conversations that lead to shared discovery of new truths and a deepening of the relationship.

DEVELOPING THE CARING SIDE

We cover this with a case study of failure, followed by a case study of success.

Failure

Now we are not all natural or nurtured carers. About 18 years ago now, when I worked for the management development centre, one of the employees was Jewish – Vanessa. She was an attractive lady, aged 38, a very gifted musician and her day job was producing videos.

It was the early 90s, when we had a recession in the UK and the management centre went through some lean times. Vanessa was made redundant, as her business line was seen as non core. At the time of our discussion, it was not a problem, as she was making more money as a consultant to the organisation, which had made her redundant, than she had been doing as an employee!

We had occasional chats, when working together and a couple of evening meals on the premises. This was the second and last. At the

Failure

previous meal, she had mentioned that she had decided to go to an analyst. At this "last supper", a few weeks later, she was telling me about it.

The key reason Vanessa had gone to an analyst was that she found managing relationships very difficult. She had one male friend and lots of casual lovers. She felt uncomfortable with being touched and touching. The shrink was helping her understand why. So far, what had been established (though she knew this already) was that her father, who had been a Professor at an African University, was a very cold and remote individual, who never gave her cuddles and with whom she could not have any viable relationship.

Her relationship with her mother had been very difficult (though cuddles were occasionally provided) because she was a survivor of Auschwitz! Two terrible realities. I intervened, after hearing this, with a suggestion.

"If I were you Vanessa, I'd give up on the shrink and force yourself every day from now on to touch a human being – a colleague, friend, relative – whomsoever appropriate and you know. It will be very difficult to start with, but, over time, it will become easier and easier and eventually it will become second nature and you will find that you'll have overcome your problem".

Vanessa literally laughed in my face at this suggestion and said. "What a ridiculous suggestion, Rupert. My analyst has told me that I am such an interesting case that it will take at least 5 years to get to the bottom of it".

At the end of those 5 years of narcissistic self-obsession, in my opinion, Vanessa would be incapable of sustaining an effective relationship with anyone – including herself.

There is a sad conclusion to this story. A couple of years ago, a colleague, who was retired and received the pensioner newsletter, advised me he read in the obituary section that Vanessa had died at the age of 53. He gave me no further details.

Failure

Joe was a senior manager in an organisation. He was a good performer, but had a poor image.

His company provided him with an executive coach to "sort him out". What the coach discovered was that the reason for the poor image was that "Joe didn't do smiles". He came across as "unfriendly" and "uncaring" – a bit on the aloof and detached side.

The coach also discovered that Joe was consistent in this detached approach in all his relationships – family, friends and social. It was not an act he had put on for the work-place.

What Joe had not consciously realised, until his coaching sessions, was just how much damage he was causing his relationships by being perceived as unfriendly and uncaring, as that was not his conscious intention. To be honest, he was just being himself and had not really thought about it at all.

So he took a decision – a brave decision. He decided he would try to come across as a more friendly kind of guy. Specifically, he decided that when he greeted a TOP in the future, he would try to put a genuine smile on his face and say something positive in a warm tone of voice.

He found it very difficult indeed. However, he was a very stubborn man. He saved himself quite a lot of heart-ache by secretly practising in front of a mirror. Eventually, he achieved success.

Much to his delight he found that the friendly greeting got an automatic positive response.

Once he had repeated success at least 20 times, he found that "he did do smiles". All his relationships improved dramatically.

BECOMING MORE LOGICAL AND PRACTICAL

❑   I am an innovative introvert – "Head in the Clouds" sort of person. I have:

  –   Forgotten I had one of my children with me, when in a

supermarket – very fortunately found before the child had become distraught – I remembered at the checkout.
– Not noticed that my wife has had a complete change in hairstyle on far too many occasions.
– Ditto with changes to the appearance of various rooms.
– Frequently "lost" keys and other important items.
– Have work colleagues asking if I am unwell when I am just thinking as I walk.
– Once cut my boss stone dead at a conference we were attending separately – days of grovelling required after that one – and so on.

❑ Fortunately I was rescued by lawyers! I won some training and development business for a large City law firm, and, as you know, spent over 13 years training and developing their lawyers.

❑ I had to become a very logical, practical and a details man as otherwise, I would have lost the business. So here is my suggestion as what to do:

– Cut out a short article from your favourite newspaper on any topic that you are very interested in.
– Study it and write down every key point that is made.
– Find the government thought or GSA (Governing Strategic Action) – the core message that is contained in the article. Sometimes it is in the heading, sometimes lost in the middle and sometimes it is in the conclusion.
– Then re-write the article in summary form with the core message first and the key points in a logical flow to "Prove the point" e.g. X must resign because of the following reasons A,B,C
– Practise, practise, practise
– Progressively go on to longer, more complex articles, where you may encounter a number of different themes, each of which has to be identified, analysed and then re-written in the "Point then prove it" logical approach.

❑ Initially, if you have a practical, logical person that you know, get them to help you do this first time round or get them to check the first output – so that you know that you have got it right first time.

Author's notes

❑ After 13 years operating frequently in the logical, practical, detailed world of lawyers, I became complete on the innovative/practical dimension.

❑ What is quite interesting is how this manifested itself. My default state was to "stay true to type" – go around with my "head in the clouds", repeating all the behaviours already covered.

❑ However, when I decided to switch or was asked to switch into the practical, here-and-now world, I would do so with complete focus and effectively.

❑ As an example, if I was given a piece of work by my wife or daughter to look at, then, fairly quickly, I could achieve the following:

– Pick up all the mistakes in spelling, punctuation and grammar.
– Identify any logical inconsistencies present.
– Identify the Governing Strategic Action (GSA), if present in the piece, or what it should be, if absent.
– Re-write the piece in the "prove the point" approach, producing a compelling case to convince the reader.

❑ Once the job was finished, then I would revert back to putting "my head in the clouds"

❑ If you are an introverted innovative and develop comfort and confidence in the practical world, you will have exactly the same experience. However, if you are an extroverted innovative, and develop practical competence, you will have developed that practical competence working with a TOP or TOPs. You will have the same result – be able to switch from animated conversations around ideas and initiatives to effective practical work with TOPs and then back to default mode. Clearly your head will rarely reach the clouds, as it is not a natural state to be in.

❑ Finally, what you are achieving by this exercise is starting at the bottom with the low-level detail items and then moving to the top – discovering the "GSA"or Governing Strategic Action. The next chapter, "Thinking and Writing with Impeccable Logic" develops your logical skills further by showing how you can start at the top and move down to the bottom.

IMPROVING CREATIVITY

I am assuming you are problem-solving on your own (as we all have to do on occasion) and you have a pen and paper. There are three rules to be religiously followed:

SEPARATE EVALUATION FROM EXPLORATION

The first step is not to try to solve the problem at all – just have ideas, only have ideas and continue until you run out of ideas. So no evaluation is permitted during exploration.

DO NOT CRITICISE YOUR OWN IDEAS

The number of times I have heard someone come up with a brilliant answer to a problem or an idea that, if they had only developed it, would have produce a great solution, but instead criticise themselves and reject it saying "it won't work", is legion.

DON'T ASSUME

Assumptions made an ASS out of U and ME.

Let us take an example of the three rules in action.

ALASKAN ELECTRICITY COMPANY

❑　The Alaskan Electricity Company faced terrible problems a number of years ago. It managed over 1000 miles of overground telegraph poles, supplying electricity to a sparse and widely scattered population in very hostile weather conditions. As a result of the terrible weather, ice and snow gathered on the overhead cables, which frequently snapped under the weight. Teams of men had to travel miles and miles to repair these cables. The costs of such operations exhausted all their profits.

❑　The company solved the problem through a group of people questioning effectively and following the three rules. These are the questions:

– Why not shake the poles?
– How do we shake the poles?
– Why not use polar bears?
– How do we motivate the bears to shake the poles?
– Why not put meat on top of the poles?
– How do we get meat on top of the poles?
– Why not use a helicopter?
– Why not forget about the bears and use the whirring blades of the helicopter to get rid of the snow and ice, before it forms?

❑ And that is what the Alaskan Electricity Company did – with considerable cost saving. Preventing the problem was, as so often the case, much more effective than trying to solve the problem

Key points

❑ Whilst it happened to be a group interaction, a single individual, provided they followed the rules, could have produced this imaginative solution to the problem.

❑ There was a logical connection between the open, exploring "how" question and the actual idea or suggestion prefaced by "why not". Logical, practical people often label themselves as not being very creative. Provided you suspend judgement, do not criticise yourself, logical people can be extremely creative.

❑ Indeed, if you accept my definition of intuition as the "*subconscious learning from experience that rests in the subconscious*", then I would argue that the learning is, in the main, a processing of the experience, i.e. thinking logically with connected steps as in the above. The subconscious brain obeys the three rules above.

❑ So, if you practise this approach to creative problem-solving (behind closed doors), you will become a quantum leaper. Just imagine that you were in the room as one of the group of the executives of the Alaskan Electricity Company and the problem had been clearly defined as: "the breaking of the wires due to the formation of ice and snow". "Right, gentlemen", says the CEO, "Let's have some ideas. If we can't solve this problem, we will go bust". You pipe up with. "Why don't we identify the trouble spots from our accurate forecasts, send a helicopter and use its whirring blades to sweep away the snow and ice before it forms? I have the figures with me and it will save us a fortune?" Awe and envy all round, a reputation as a creative genius, as well as a sound egg, and promotion guaranteed.

❑ Clearly criticism would have killed the solution stone dead. Those who criticise always have to give a reason. So we would have had comments along the lines of:

– "Why not shake the poles" – "what a stupid impractical idea?"
– "Why not use polar bears" – "how ridiculous. I have done my research and there are 3 million poles and 650 polar bears"
– "Why not put meat on top of the poles" – "How stupid can you get. The polar bears would smash the wires in the attempt to get the meat."
– I now develop the suggestion of "Do not assume" more actively and creatively, i.e. be creative on assumptions

Be creative on assumptions

❑ I am sure that many of you will have come across what are termed, "Lateral Thinking Questions". Because of the prevalence of "the one right answer" mentality, they were designed for there to be one right answer. You were supposed to suddenly, magically quantum leap sideways or laterally to find this one right answer.

❑ An example is: "A man sold his dog, and was killed on the way home". One effective way of providing a number of answers is to be creative on assumptions, i.e. say to yourself: "What are all the assumptions I could conceivably make, when considering this problem". Being creative on assumptions will produce a range of different answers. You will achieve what is termed "break-through" thinking. So let us look at the range of answers, which is not exhaustive.

– It could have been a very valuable dog, and the man was mugged (and died) on the way home for the money.

– It could have been a large, angry dog, and escaped from his new owners, and carried out a fatal revenge attack on his former master.

– It could have been a particular breed of dog, e.g. a husky, and the man had sold the lead dog of his sled and had fallen in a crevasse and died, or a guide dog, as his master was blind, and the blind man had been run over on the way home.

– It could have been his wife's dog, which she adored much, much more than hubbie and so she shot her husband. [This not strictly permissible, due to the fact that it was "his" dog - but no criticism rules OK. In any case, it is a good idea not to define a problem too closely, if you want to avoid missing out on potentially fantastic solutions. The problem would have been better put: "A man sold a dog and was killed on the way home", in which case there are many more solutions.]

– If you study the phrasing, there is nothing to stop you interpreting the sentence as to mean that the dog was killed on the way home – run over, eaten, killed by another dog and so on.

– You can argue that there is no connection between the two and then come up with as many answers as you like as to why a man should be killed on the way home!

❑ Finally, you can use a variation of the "being creative on assumptions" technique to be creative on possible causes of a given problem.

Identify the cause; do not solve the effect or outcome

❑ A major problem with problem-solving is that people see an outcome, e.g. well above average sickness in a business area, and treat that as the problem. How we reduce sickness? We toughen up the rules to reduce it. Problem solved. No, more problems created. The sickness was a symptom, effect or outcome of the real problem. The real problem (in a real case) was that the newly appointed business head was an out-an-out bully, who had totally demotivated his staff. Before he arrived, the sick leave was, actually, a little bit below average. It had steadily risen, unnoticed, until it was so statistically significant that alarm bells had risen and a knee-jerk reaction contemplated. The solution, which was taken, was to let him go.

❑ Now a classic problem for most companies, at some time, is that sales revenues start falling. The knee-jerk "solve the symptom" mentality is very logical. If sales revenues are falling, we must cut costs. Staff are our biggest costs, so we must shed staff.

❑ Let us apply the "being creative on assumptions" technique in the guise of the following question: "What could be all the possible reasons why sales have started falling?"

❑ The following is not exhaustive, but by way of example. I call it the Why/Why approach as you get tiers of causes, as we can see below.

Level 1

What are all the possible reasons why sales are falling? (FIRST WHY)

- Declining Market
- Competitor cut prices
- Quality of product has deteriorated
- Sales effectiveness reduced

You pause at level 1 and examine the facts. Suppose the market is not declining, no competitor has cut prices, and the quality of the product is above standard (as it has been over the last few years). So you know that falling sales revenue is due to the fact that sales effectiveness has reduced. [This assumes that you have been exhaustive in your level 1 causes]. So you move to the second "why" at level 2.

Level 2

What are all the possible reasons for sales effectiveness to be reduced (SECOND WHY)

- Effectiveness of training reduced due to recent outsourcing.
- Recent personnel changes in the top team have impacted negatively on morale and hence performance.

– Remuneration package becoming less competitive, increasing staff turnover.

Research will then be necessary to establish what is the actual cause or causes. Once they have been uncovered, then you come up with all the possible solutions, using your creative thinking skills.

Author's note
By far the most effective way of improving individual creativity is through being part of a high-performing team. Such teams produce what is termed "creative synergy", i.e. the quality of creative thinking is higher than any individual can achieve and the total number of ideas exceeds the sum of individual creative contributions. How you can achieve this as team-builder is covered in Chapter 8, "Build and Effective Team Very Rapidly".

IMPROVING FLEXIBLE AND PLANNING SKILLS

❑ Any project can be completed to a high standard ahead of schedule by both Flexibles and Organisers. We will take, by way of example, a project with a six-month deadline. The following four principles need to be followed:

– Set the final deadline at least a fortnight early and mentally treat it as the ultimate deadline.
– Break the project down into smaller, discrete, manageable chunks, i.e. a series of sequentially linked mini-projects.
– Set interim milestones and deadlines, i.e. what you have to achieve by when for each mini-project.
– Treat each deadline mentally as if it was a final deadline for the mini-project.

❑ We look at the benefits for Flexibles, followed by the benefits for Organisers.

BENEFITS FOR FLEXIBLES

❑ Flexibles are *"spontaneous, remain open to new information and last minute options"* and *"work with imminent deadlines as they generate most creativity and energy".*

❑ As a result, with a single project deadline, they often miss it, which is a "career regressive move" in the work-place.

❑ By breaking the project down into, say, 10 mini-projects, logically and sequentially connected, Flexibles now have 10 deadlines to miss.

❑ Provided Flexibles treat each deadline as serious and exercise a degree of self-discipline, then, by the end of the project, the slippage on the final deadline will be, say, a week. As this final deadline is 2 weeks ahead of the real deadline, they have completed the project one week ahead of schedule.

❑ They will then receive a comment from their boss along the lines of: "Well done indeed. I had not realised that you had become a brilliant planner and maintained your usual high quality standards."

❑ Because you are endlessly trying to discipline yourself, which comes naturally to organisers, through the harnessing the power of SPO, eventually you become more organised. When you fill in the NPQ again, if you had a 3 before, you will find that you now score yourself 2.

BENEFITS FOR ORGANISERS

❑ Organisers *"take an organized, planned and structured approach"* and *"allow plenty of time to plan and focus, and avoid the stress of last minute deadlines."*

❑ As a result, organisers make their decisions too quickly and wallow in a mess of detail. They also suffer the stress caused by Robbie Burns saying "the plans of mice and men gang aft agley". Unexpected changes (or exogenous shocks) are inevitable in the world of change, in which we all live.

❑ By breaking the project down into 10 mini-projects, they can avoid unnecessary detail early on. They can also deal retrospectively with the inevitable exogenous shocks.

❑ As they are likely to be a week ahead of their own planned schedule (and hence 3 weeks ahead of the actual deadline), they will have time to fine-tune the final output to take into account the latest information prevailing or exogenous shock that has occurred.

❑ They will deliver the project on time and two weeks early in real-time. They will receive a comment from their boss along the lines of: "Well done indeed. I have always known that you are a brilliant planner. The quality of the end product is outstanding".

❑ As Organisers are frequently exposing themselves to less detail and more change, they are harnessing the power of SPO. Eventually, they will become more Flexible. When you fill in the NPQ again, if you had a 3 before, you will find that you now score yourself a 2.

Chapter 5
Think and Write with Impeccable Knowledge

INTRODUCTION

❑ Jon Moynihan, when CEO of PA Consulting Group, gained a competitive edge in the market-place by training all the consultants in what was referred to as "Top-Down" thinking – the ability to think and write with impeccable logic.

❑ I was one of a team of partners and management consultants, trained by John Moynihan to downstream the day and a half programme he designed.

❑ The advantages for you of learning the methodology are that you will be the first to get the point and get to the point, and be very persuasive indeed. All your presentations and written communication will be clear, concise and compelling.

❑ We start by setting out and exemplifying the principles of Top-Down thinking with the action-oriented header "Improving leadership".

❑ We then develop key points. We conclude by considering how to make outstanding presentations and apply Top-Down principles to the content.

IMPROVING LEADERSHIP

"Have something to say and say it as clearly as you can."
Matthew Arnold

SITUATION

We describe the situation or context. This is the background to the thinking or writing. Here we have:

Managers carry out a leadership role for their staff.

COMPLICATION

Introduce the complication or reason to write or think.

The organisation realises that it is important to improve the "bottom line" so that the "bar is raised", i.e. the performance of those in a leadership role is improved.

KEY QUESTION

Decide on the key question that naturally arises in the reader's (thinker's) mind as a result of the complication.

How are we going to improve the performance of those in a leadership role?

ANSWER OR GOVERNING STRATEGIC ACTION (GSA)

We produce a template as to what effective leaders do.

KEY QUESTION THAT NATURALLY COMES INTO THE READER'S MIND

What do effective leaders do?

PROVIDE THE ANSWERS AT THE KEYLINE – THE ACTION DRIVERS

1. Develop themselves.
2. Lead by example.
3. Put the follower's work into context.
4. Develop their followers.
5. Provide support to their followers.

ASK THE QUESTION THAT NATURALLY COMES INTO THE READER'S MIND FOR EACH ACTION AREA AND ANSWER IT

Looking at each action driver in turn, we have:

1. Develop themselves
How?

- ☐ Think about their leadership role.
- ☐ Develop self-awareness.
- ☐ Focus on their followers.
- ☐ Implement plans to improve.

2. Lead by example
What?

- ☐ Are honest and encourage honesty.
- ☐ Acknowledge shortcomings and mistakes.
- ☐ Display confidence and commitment.
- ☐ Create team spirit.

3. Put the follower's work into context
How?

- ☐ Develop and share the vision and values.
- ☐ Create the big picture.
- ☐ Agree clear goals and objectives.
- ☐ Monitor and review performance.

4. Develop their followers
How?

- ☐ Provide direction and guidance.
- ☐ Coach.
- ☐ Give feedback.
- ☐ Provide more challenging work.

5. Provide support to their followers
How?

❏ Are available and approachable.
❏ Encourage and praise.
❏ Listen and are receptive to ideas.
❏ Are a safety net.

Author's note
I produced this template as the result of years of research. It was adopted by a global organisation.

KEY POINTS

❏ All the headers, sub-headers and points made should be "active" or action-orientated. Because of the power of SPO, the reader reaches the conclusion that you are a pro-active, action-oriented individual – just the right message to get across. It is also intrinsically more compelling. The topic header "Leadership" does not do nearly as much for the reader as "Improving leadership" or "Improve your leadership".

❏ You may or may not have consciously noticed the deliberate repetition of key action-oriented points in headers and sub-headers in this book. There was also a lot of repetition in the above. Ideally, you want to repeat a key message three times. After the third time, as you know, it has sunk in at the subconscious level.

❏ The "situation" should always be a statement of fact that does not generate any controversy at this early stage.

❏ Without a "complication", there is no need to write in the first place.

❏ The GSA or Governing Strategic Action (or overarching theme) determines the strategic level of entry. It is critically important that you choose a GSA at the appropriate strategic level. One of the reasons culture change efforts have failed is because a GSA "We must change culture" is too high for effective strategic action.

❑ Your entry level can also be too low. As we have already seen, if the situation is "our revenues are falling" and the GSA is "We must cut staff costs", you have answered the wrong question. The methodology is flexible enough to accommodate this – provided you ask the right "Key Question". So, funnily enough, you need to develop your creative thinking skills to be able to generate the right GSA. It is often helpful to have quite a general key question., e.g:

> **Situation:** Our revenues are falling.
> **Complication:** This will impact negatively on our profitability.
> **Key Question:** How do we solve this problem?
> **GSA:** We discover all the possible reasons why our revenues are falling.

❑ In many, many real-life work-related situations, there is no need for a situation, complication, or key question as the GSA is obvious – the next section on delivering outstanding presentations is a case in point.

❑ The action drivers at the Keyline are more commonly referred to as agenda items or core themes – hence the universal application of this methodology to any communication that has an issue to be considered or point to be made.

❑ The GSA (also, as we know, referred to as the Governing Thought) is THE POINT, i.e. the highest level action required. This, in simple parlance, is the conclusion. As you know, in many communications, it comes at the beginning, the middle or the end. On some occasions, it is missed completely. On those occasions, when it has been reached with a flourish at the end, the sub-points (detail items) that justify it have been made in an arbitrary, scatter-gun approach, and many key sub-points have been omitted. The reader is unconvinced or bewildered or both.

❑ This is why the research on outstanding negotiators pointed out that you need to agree the high-level "common theme" first and avoid the detail and why Edward de Bono suggested that you should not define any problem too narrowly, i.e. enter at too low a level.

❑ "Top-Down" thinking is, in fact, a very effective way of

"negotiating" with or "persuading" TOP, when discussing an issue. This is because you base your argument on "questions that naturally flow in TOP's mind", and then use "impeccable logic" to prove THE POINT.

MAKE OUTSTANDING PRESENTATIONS
In this section, we cover:

- ❑ When do we give a presentation?
- ❑ What are the requirements for an effective presenter?
- ❑ How should we present?
- ❑ How do we plan?
- ❑ How to use Top-Down thinking effectively for the content?
- ❑ How to deliver the presentation?
- ❑ How to deal with questions?

WHEN DO WE GIVE A PRESENTATION?

- ❑ In marketing our services to internal or external clients.
- ❑ At conferences or seminars.
- ❑ In briefing colleagues.
- ❑ Almost all the time!

WHAT ARE THE REQUIREMENTS OF AN EFFECTIVE PRESENTER?
The requirements for an effective presenter are to have the confidence to be yourself and being able to deliver both your message and yourself. Model presenters are:

- ❑ Confident.
- ❑ Relaxed.
- ❑ Animated.
- ❑ In control.
- ❑ Interesting.
- ❑ Sincere.
- ❑ Believe in their own subject.
- ❑ Gain audience rapport.

HOW SHOULD WE PRESENT?
Body language

❑ Good body language is natural. The effects include: to support what is being said (hand gestures/facial expressions); to involve the audience (eye contact/nods); to convey enthusiasm and sincerity (smiles, movements) and to help keep the audience awake. It is hypnotic to watch someone in apparent rigor mortis!

❑ Poor body language is unnatural, typically stiff or involving unnatural movements, betraying the speaker's nerves. The effects include: to distract the audience from what is being said and/or to send them to sleep!

❑ The table of do's and don'ts for all parts of the body is set out on the next page.

	DO's	DON'Ts
Hands/Arms	❑ Use them. ❑ When not using, try holding hands together lightly with elbows bent.	❑ Play with pens/rings and so on. ❑ Put hands in pockets. ❑ Clench anything.
Torso	❑ Upright. ❑ Open to audience.	❑ Slouch. ❑ Swing/rock.
Legs	❑ Natural movement according to situation. ❑ If standing still, legs should be shoulder-length apart, i.e. balanced.	❑ Pace/hop/rock. ❑ Clean shoes on trousers.

	DO's	DON'Ts
Eyes	❑ Make eye contact with ALL of your audience 95% of the time. ❑ Sweep round and keep the eye contact to a couple of seconds max.	❑ Make robotic head movements. ❑ Look at ceiling/floor. ❑ Exclude people at edges. ❑ Stare. ❑ Look at visual aid.
Face/Mouth	❑ Be expressive, relaxed and confident. ❑ Smile.	❑ Look miserable. ❑ Lose all emotion.

Voice
The model presenter, in fact, has more emphasis in his/her speech than normal speech. However, the overall impression received by the listener is that it is natural. The five main elements of our speech are:

Pitch
In an average presentation, this is very frequently monotone or squeaky – betraying nerves. In natural speech, pitch varies. Put your enthusiasm and interest in your topic into your voice. You tend to need more variation in pitch in order to maintain audience concentration. Be careful not to overlay a rhythm of:

❑   Boredom.
❑   Apology.
❑   Arrogance.

Volume

❑   The average presenter speaks with less confidence – a mixture of "cool" and passive – than in normal speech, usually with less volume.

❑   Turn up the volume a little.

❑   Be definite, punchy and "cool".

Pace

❑   The average presenter has a tendency to speak too quickly. However, a staccato delivery of points is tedious. A brisk presentation is fine as long as:

    – You are clear/people can hear.
    – Pauses are used.

❑   Varying pace changes audience perception:

    – Faster = more energy/enthusiasm/suggests assumed pre-knowledge.
    – Slower = adds emphasis.

❑   Distinguish rate of word delivery and rate of idea delivery. You must give sufficient time for each idea to be absorbed, before moving on.

Pauses

Average speakers omit pauses or make "um..." "er..." pauses only. Pauses are part of natural speech. Furthermore, they:

❑   Allow thinking space (for them and you).

❑   Add weight to what has been said.

❑   Re-gather audience attention/create anticipation.

❑   Allow you to pick up sign language (nods/frowns etc.), i.e. the "did-you-get-that" pause.

Diction

❑   Don't mumble!

❑   Talk clearly and to your audience.

HOW TO PLAN THE PRESENTATION?

❏   Put first things first. So ask yourself:

Why am I doing this presentation? Who are the audience?	Marketing, training, briefing… Status, background, nationalities, numbers…
What does the audience already know?	People don't listen to much of what they already know.
What are the key messages that I want to deliver/action that I want them to follow?	These are crucial. They must be relevant to the audience.
How formal/informal is the presentation?	Do you know the participants? Check venue size, layouts and so on.

❏   Above all, ask: "What's in it for the listener?" If the presentation does not address their aims/needs, they won't listen.

HOW TO USE TOP-DOWN THINKING EFFECTIVELY FOR THE CONTENT

This presentation has become standard throughout one of my former global clients, when presenting to prospective clients. I will set out the presentation in terms of slide content and then make a few key points. I have not added any appropriate visuals.

Slide 1
Serving our clients

Slide 2
Serving our clients

❏   Agree needs.

- ❏ Meet needs.
- ❏ Deepen relationship.
- ❏ Develop long-term partnership.

Slide 3
Agree needs

- ❏ Understand business/cultural context.
- ❏ Develop empathy.
- ❏ Ensure own expertise recognised.
- ❏ Develop thinking.
- ❏ Demonstrate value to be added.
- ❏ Agree standards.

Slide 4
Meet needs

- ❏ Display commitment.
- ❏ Ensure agreed standards met.
- ❏ Pay attention to detail.
- ❏ Demonstrate cultural fit.

Slide 5
Deepen relationship

- ❏ Ask for feedback.
- ❏ Implement improvements.
- ❏ Deliver repeat business.
- ❏ Obtain referrals.
- ❏ Identify additional needs.
- ❏ Add to core services.

Slide 6
Develop Long-Term Partnership

- ❏ Expand personal network of relationships with the client.
- ❏ Introduce colleagues into the expanded network.

❑ Develop mutual problem solving.
❑ Expand breadth and depth of needs met.

Final slide (7)
Serving our clients

❑ Agree needs.
❑ Meet needs.
❑ Deepen relationship.
❑ Develop long-term partnership.

KEY POINTS

❑ The questions are all "how" – kept implicit. This enables client pull rather than product push. "Why" questions lead to product push. "You should use us because we are such lovely people and cheap at half the price".

❑ The situation, complication, and key question are taken as read. The GSA pops out immediately.

❑ The MECE rule is followed.

– This means that no point made should be duplicated (points should be Mutually Exclusive) and all the answers should be provided to a given question (points should be Collectively Exhaustive) – hence MECE.

– This is a difficult rule to implement. It is the yardstick by which you ensure you have created a watertight, logically consistent and compelling presentation or any piece of writing/thinking.

– If you break the Mutually Exclusive element, it distracts the listener. *"Didn't she make the same point in an earlier section?* (For instance) *Why do I need to "agree standards" when meeting needs, when I have already been told to "agree standards" when agreeing needs?*) The inconsistency niggles away (subconsciously) at the listener and not only distracts them as you move forward, but they begin to lose faith in you.

– If you break the Collectively Exhaustive element, the listener may stop paying attention as the fact that a key reason (if a "why" question) or a key action (if a "how" question) is not there will begin to distract and cause loss of faith, as before.

– Assuming in the slide on "Meet needs" there was no reference to "ensure agreed standards met", some listeners may well start saying to themselves (subconsciously): *"We have just covered how to "agree needs" and now we have just finished how to "meet needs"* and there is no reference to making sure that the standards agreed are met. That can't be right."

❑ It is important to recognise that you can choose the level of detail in any Top-Down communication, e.g. under "meet needs", when stating "display commitment", the question that naturally pops into the reader's or listener's mind is another "how". For a detailed written report, this may be necessary. In a presentation, this gives an opportunity to expand each point or sub-theme as a speaker. It also avoids cluttering up the slides with "information overload" and prevents you speaking from the slides rather than to the audience.

❑ Typically, two levels are usually right – this indicates that you have "pitched your communication at the right level". With three or more, it becomes too complex for the reader to follow and indicates that your entry level is too high, e.g. we must change culture. Conversely, if there is only one level that flows naturally from your GSA to produce the agenda items, it indicates you have entered at too low a level, e.g. we must cut staff costs.

❑ If you look at the second level sub-points, you will notice that the follow up questions are trivial or even unnecessary, e.g. "expand network" or "develop mutual problem-solving" or "identify additional needs". This is a sure indication that you have got it right first time.

HOW TO DELIVER THE PRESENTATION?
The beginning
You

❑ Professional in appearance (your appearance should not be a distraction) but comfortable.

- ❏ Wear a jacket, which will enable you to clip on a microphone, if using one.
- ❏ Be careful with:

  - Perfume/after shave.
  - Hair falling in your face.
  - Skimpy or see-through clothing.

Introduction

- ❏ Who you are and something establishing why you – i.e. credibility.
- ❏ Do not go OTT on your expertise. This sounds like showing off.
- ❏ If someone else is to introduce you, check what they are going to say.

Funnel

- ❏ Something to focus audience/capture interest, e.g:

  - "Gee whiz" statistic/fact.
  - A "big issue"/something topical/in news.

- ❏ Ensure that the funnel is genuinely relevant to the subject. Jokes are very high risk and best avoided.

Presentation title

- ❏ Introduce the title (GSA) without addition/bias/conclusion, e.g. "I am going to talk to you about how we serve our clients". Using the word "how" ensures that you have planted the question that "naturally flows into the listener's mind"!
- ❏ This is far, far, far better than the value laden approach: "I am here to tell you how fantastic we are at serving our clients" or "Why we are better than all our competitors" or, perish the thought, the product push approach: "I am here to tell you why we have such fantastic products (services) to offer you."

❑ The sheer quality, power and relevance to your audience of your presentation will, through that wonderful process of subconscious psychological osmosis, lead the audience to reach all these conclusions without you having to utter a single word on the three subjects.

Agenda

As mentioned, this is simply the first level themes that flow from the core theme or GSA.

❑ Do NOT address "low-level" concerns. The typical advice given by "experts" is that, before you start the presentation, you address such concerns as:

– How long will the presentation last.
– What happens after the presentation, e.g. lunch/visit round the premises.
– What the hand-outs are, as you plonk them down on the desk near you.
– Your policy on receiving questions, e.g. "allows interruptions" or "receive at end".

Do not address such concerns – go straight into the presentation, having introduced yourself or having being introduced. Once you start, any low-level concerns will disappear completely.

❑ Two critical points:

1. You want the audience to get involved and fully engaged. If a member of the audience is so involved, they will ask a question. In fact, after making a specific point – ask in a friendly tone of voice if there any questions. If you create a situation where there is "discussion leading to discovery" then you have succeeded. If you can achieve this when making a formal presentation to an interviewing panel, then you have got the job.
2. As you now know, research findings indicate that members of the audience remember least if they just listen (hence the beauty of

involving them in discussion) and are told they will receive hand-outs at the end. Keep your hand-outs well hidden under a convenient table or desk.

Author's note

The key to a perfect beginning is not to rush it. Your nerves will settle down quickly, but be sure that you know exactly what you're going to say during the first couple of minutes.

The middle

As you have already structured your information in a logical and compelling way, anticipating the questions the audience (implicitly) asks, you simply follow it.

Amplify each point

❑   When amplifying each key point at each level:

– Draw on "real life" situations – your own experience or current events.
– Use examples that are relevant.
– Beware company speak, abbreviations, flowery language or jargon.

❑   No more than six sub-themes per agenda item/theme. This is because research has indicated that we can remember up to 5 items, then our memory starts tailing off after 6 and, above that, we start forgetting one or more items. Also, we tend to remember the first two or three and the ending item. So, if one or more are forgotten, they are after the middle and before the end. This means that, in any written communication, you place any weaker points in the appropriate place. (All your points will be very strong, of course!)

Language

❑   Use the power of three and alliteration, e.g. "*I came, I saw, I conquered.*"

❏ Remember you will have a mix of Visuals, Auditories and Kinaesthetics in your audience. So use the appropriate phrases set out in Chapter 2. At the least, remember to vary so that you use the words "see", "hear" and "feel".

Maintain interest

❏ Keep it punchy
❏ Use visuals.
❏ Ask the audience questions.
❏ Involve the audience.

End

❏ You will receive a spontaneous round of applause. People will break out into animated discussions with you and in small groups.
❏ You will have to call them to order to advise the next step and give out the hand-outs, they had completely forgotten existed.

KEY POINTS TO CONCLUDE

❏ If you practice this 21 times, you will think automatically with impeccable logic.
❏ You will therefore increase your intuition or "gut feel", as a result, whether Controller or Carer. Quoting from the previous chapter from the "improving creativity" section: *"If you accept my definition that intuition or "gut feel" is the subconscious processing of experience by the subconscious that rests in the subconscious, then once this way of thinking has become a habit, the subconscious becomes much more efficient in processing those experiences and so you develop more intuition."*

Chapter 6

Succeed in the Political World

INTRODUCTION
In this key chapter, we look at how you can:

❑ Harness the power of persuasion
❑ Ensure your boss, however difficult he or she is currently perceived, becomes a champion for your career.
❑ Take advantage of a critical research finding to improve your prospects for promotion.

HARNESS THE POWER OF PERSUASION

❑ The key to effective persuasion is to apply the PBA rule. I discovered the rule in 1992 and wrote about it in my first published book: "The Power of Persuasion – how to improve your performance and leadership skills" (1992).
❑ PBA stands for Perceived Balance of Advantage. The rule is that: *"Whenever TOP perceives a balance of personal advantage in the proposition you are putting forward, then TOP will say 'yes'."* There are two key implications (see overleaf).

PULL NOT PUSH

The problems with push

Martin was an Extrovert Controlling Practical Organiser. He had had a good career. By his early 30s he had reached a middle management position. The CDMU (Core Decision-Making Unit) was male dominated. This was just as well, as Martin was, not to put too fine a point on it, a Male Chauvinist Pig.

Now Male Chauvinist Pigs put on a very good act of hiding it in the workplace or so they think. [They don't bother at home.] They never realise that all women see through it in an instant.

Over time, a few women were appointed to senior positions and his card was being progressively marked, without him knowing it, of course. What plateaued him completely were the winds of change that have blown into gales throughout nearly all companies.

Being practical, and having never attempted to develop his non-preferred innovative side, he was "dead in the water".

Around the age of 35, he woke up to the reality, helped by his wife, who was the Sally mentioned in the second chapter. Unfortunately, he never got past the semi-final stage of any selection process.

There was at least one woman on all the interviewing panels. Additionally, he believed that proving to his potential new employers that he was the best thing since sliced bread, i.e. pushing himself as the perfect product was the one right answer. The combination was lethal.

Unfortunately for Martin, eventually he had to side-ways move to a different sector. He had to jump before he was pushed. He also lost his wife and two young children. Sally divorced him.

KNOW WHEN YOU HAVE WON

❑　　The number of times I have witnessed a persuader successfully persuade TOP, and then blow it, are legion. What happens, typically, is that they have rehearsed a series of arguments to get TOP to agree.

❑   They accidentally hit a Hot Spot for TOP (applied PBA without knowing it), who says "Yes". They don't hear it! They carry on with the whole set of arguments, usually introducing one that is perceived negatively by TOP. TOP ends up saying "No".

❑   We conclude this section with a case study of success – John gets the career move he desired.

John gets the career move he desired

A group of executives on a senior executive development programme were carrying out persuasion role-plays, dealing with important work-related issues. The objective was to learn more about how to be persuasive and to increase the probability of successful outcomes, when they had to do it for real.

One persuader, John, wanted to persuade his boss, played by Gerald, to allow him to move up North to expand a business line, which research had showed would be welcomed by customers and would make a good profit for his company.

The first attempt was a disaster. The persuader was rather full of himself, very strong on the benefits to the customer and the company, which he assumed would be clinchers, and occasionally was verbally aggressive. This was despite the fact that he had briefed the persuadee as to the key drivers of his boss – developing his empire, building his reputation and personal prestige and avoiding any significant change.

The project, as presented, represented major change, reduced his boss's empire, and the key message that emerged was just how good a move it would be for the persuader! The person playing the role of the boss – the persuadee – played it well, and inevitably turned the project down.

All five of us had a chat. (There were two other executives, acting as observers and commentators until it was their turn.) The PBA rule was introduced. John spent some time formulating his strategy and the role-play was re-run. It was successful. I was advised by John a few weeks later that he also been successful with his real boss in the real world. Let us look at the conversation, encapsulating the new approach.

John gets the career move he desired

Gerald: "Come in and sit down, John. I can give you no more than half-an-hour, as I have a meeting with Callum (the MD) at 11. What do you want?"

John: "Thanks very much for seeing me, Gerald. I want your permission for me to move to Edinburgh to open up the Scottish mobile phone market."

Gerald: "Why on earth do you want to do that? You are doing very well down here, your existing business is expanding, and you form an important part of my team. I don't want to lose you."

John: "You won't lose me Gerald. I think it is important that there is continuity. So I suggest that I report in directly to you, as now, but also have a dotted line into Tim, the Northern Region General Manager."

Gerald: "I see. That makes sense – but there is still going to be a lot of disruption. To begin with, I would need to find someone to take over your role."

John: "Hardly any disruption at all, Gerald. I have already had a word with Personnel, and they have one or two internal candidates, who they think you would approve of. In any case, I would not move until the new man was in place, and I had handed over the reins. We mustn't rush into these things."

Gerald: "Oh! I agree completely. But there is always a chance that the business will fail, and I don't want that to happen."

John: "We have carried out detailed research – the market is ripe and will expand rapidly. We will be first in and gain a competitive edge. We have succeeded down South against tough competition.We will succeed even more up North with no competition, and we will all benefit, politically speaking, from being part of a success story."

Gerald: "I see, I see. You may well have something in this new project. I am in favour, in principle."

John: "That's great, Gerald. I'll give you all the research papers and business plan by the end of the week, and get onto Personnel straightaway, so that you can look at the CVs of suitable candidates to replace me. Thanks very much for your support."

ANALYSIS

❑   John had to make a fundamental shift in attitude and approach to be successful. He was very much a "can-do" person, keen to make things happen quickly. In terms of natural strengths, he was an Extroverted Innovative Controller.

❑   However, once he starting viewing the proposition from his boss's perspective – put his PBA hat on – he realised that he had to be conservative – and plan accordingly. His boss was an Extrovert Practical Controller.

❑   What is more, he was pro-active in developing strategies to accommodate his boss's conservatism and cater for his key drivers before the actual meeting. Specifically:

– Allowing his boss to remain his boss (knowing full well that out of sight would be out of mind) so that the boss's empire would expand.
– Liaising with Personnel so the replacement issue was covered.
– Confirming the new man would be in place, before leaving.
– Focusing the benefits on enhancing his boss's credibility and personal reputation, but in a subtle "we" approach.
– Taking responsibility for all subsequent actions to minimise the impact of the change on his boss.

❑   Another very effective approach was the use of language that mirrored his boss's own practical nature. Specifically:

– "I think it is important there is continuity."
– "Hardly any disruption at all."
–   "We mustn't rush into these things" (which received enthusiastic agreement from Gerald!)
– "We have carried out detailed research."

❑   This situation is not one where you, as the person doing the persuading, are full of open questions (John asked no questions at all), but where you have thought through all the angles from TOP's perspective before you meet, implemented any necessary actions before the meeting (e.g. liaising with Personnel), ensured you talk the same language as the persuadee during the meeting and listened effectively throughout.

❏ Incidentally, before the actual meeting, he had produced the research papers and business plan to provide at the meeting – a helpful hint provided by the guy playing his boss.

❏ Gerald played the role of the boss very convincingly indeed. This was because he was also an Extrovert Practical Controller, and had the highest status in the group!

❏ There had been a certain degree of "personality clash" between these two at the start of that particular programme. Fortunately, I used the recipe to build a high-performing team in 4 hours early on, as I did on all the management development programmes I ran. This nipped any potential clashes in the bud. The recipe is covered in detail in Chapter 8, "Transform your Team-Building Competence".

CONCLUDING KEY POINT

❏ You have, in Chapter 2, a list of all the activities covering the 4 sets of polar opposite natural strengths, dispositions or bents. You also have a description of the different beliefs and language used. In Chapter 4 you have all the strategies to develop competence in the non-preferred areas.

❏ You are, therefore, in a position to ensure that you can effectively close the gap that may exist between you and any TOP you want to persuade on all four key dimensions to life.

MAKE THE BOSS THE CHAMPION FOR YOUR CAREER

❏ If the key decision-taker on your career is the boss's boss, it is vital that you find that out swiftly and make sure that he or she also becomes a champion for you career. Here we focus on your boss.

❏ You will be fully aware that it is "career regressive" to tell your boss that you don't like him. We are assuming that you do not like your boss.

❏   Unfortunately, thanks to Iceberg's 90/10 rule (Subconscious rules OK), you tell your boss that you don't like him without speaking a word. So, to have an effective relationship with your boss, you have to stop disliking him and start liking him.

❏   On numerous development programmes, I have carried out the "good boss"/ "bad boss" exercise. One group(s) is sent away to determine, by sharing real-life experience, what are all the destructive actions bad bosses take that have demotivated them. The other group focuses on all the constructive actions good bosses take to motivate them. Needless to say the list is very complete for "bad bosses" and somewhat patchy for "good bosses".

❏   A typical list, which it is just possible you might recognise, contains the following:

   – Does not listen to you.
   – Fails to delegate or simply dumps.
   – Shows no interest in you.
   – Does not respect you.
   – Gives negative feedback to a third party.
   – Does not give praise, when praise is due.
   – Criticises you in front of others.
   – Takes personal credit for your ideas.
   – Is always taking control.
   – Bullies you – verbal abuse and shouting at you.
   – Does not give you the tools to do the job.
   – Does not keep you informed.
   – Does not set clear objectives.
   – Show favouritism – one rule for one, another for others.
   – Is intransigent and closed minded.

❏   When we are abused by our boss, we, naturally, take it personally and get very upset, stressed or even depressed as a result. So I ask, innocently, why they take it personally. The typical reply is because the abuse is personal!

❏   Then, the next question is to ask if only they, or do all members of the team, get it in the neck from their boss. Nearly all the delegates reply that it is the whole team. (On the very rare occasions that it is only one, I do some personal counselling. It is an early warning for me that they should start seriously thinking about leaving the company.)

❑ So next, I ask them: "*Why do you think your boss behaves so badly?*" Typically at least one, if not more, of the group, will, after a pause, reply along the lines: "*Because the poor bastard is in worse shit than we are – far too many change projects, tight deadlines, demanding clients and so on and so on.*" The hatred is now beginning to slip away.

❑ Next comes the question: "*Imagine you are stressed out of your mind, and have been for weeks, then putting hands on hearts, which of the fifteen listed behaviours, would you not be capable of carrying out yourselves*". The penny has started to drop.

❑ Finally, I get them to focus on all the good qualities of their actual bosses and try to learn them by heart – produce affirmative statements for their boss. Affirmative statements are simply statements of fact, incorporating all the key skills and qualities that any TOP has exhibited in the past, set out with three lines of prose, each mentioning three connected qualities or skills to harness the power of 3, when repeating them.

❑ As we were not covering natural dispositions on nearly all those programmes, I missed a trick. I should have got them to work out the set of natural strengths of their boss and themselves (which you can now do) and see the extent and degree of difference. Then they would have realised that their dislike was also driven by difference or "personality clashes".

❑ Well, you know what to do. If necessary, you will have to change your attitude before trying to change your actions. When and if that has been achieved, then you have all the tools from this book to make your boss the champion for your career.

TAKE ADVANTAGE OF A CRITICAL RESEARCH FINDING TO IMPROVE YOUR CAREER

❑ In the early 1990s, research was carried out by the Head of IBM(UK) into what were the factors in large organisations that underpinned the career path – enabling regular promotions to achieve a successful career – and what percentage contribution they made to gaining that promotion. There were three:

1. Your performance contributed a miserly 10%.
2. Your image contributed 30%.
3. Your exposure (the size of network to whom you exposed your image) contributed a massive 60%.

❑ The smaller the organisation, the greater will be the contribution of performance. Nevertheless, developing the right image and ensuring it is exposed in the right places will be a critical key to unlock career success. As an outplacement consultant once said to me, *"No network, no job"*. *"It is not what you know, but who you know"*. We look at developing a powerful positive image and ensuring effective exposure.

DEVELOP A POWERFUL, POSITIVE IMAGE

❑ You develop your ability to be a "cool" communicator and will walk the corridors of power with powerful body language that, because, "first impressions count", will convey your confidence and calm authority before you speak a word.
❑ You observe the way the highest flyer in the organisation dresses and replicate it. This point is NOT gender irrelevant!

ENSURE EFFECTIVE EXPOSURE
The strategies to achieve success have been set out in Chapter 4.

❑ Extroverts need to develop their introverted side so that they harness the power of focussed one-on-one conversations with key players.
❑ Introverts need to develop their extroverted side. They start by playing to their strengths, joining odd-numbered groups and having effective one-on-one conversations with key players. Over time, by repetition of success, they become comfortable in group situations – psychologically choose to attend, rather than avoid,

the important networking opportunities, with which they are presented. Finally they are pro-active and create these networking opportunities.

Chapter 7

Transform Your Leadership Skills

INTRODUCTION

"Contains practical wisdom and psychological insights that together are indispensible to becoming an effective leader." *Miles Emley, Master of the Worshipful Company of Leathersellers, Chairman of St. Ives plc (1993-2011).*

In this chapter, we:

❑ Demonstrate how the Natural Strengths Questionnaire (NSQ) enables you to determine your natural preference for management or leadership and the difference between management and leadership. Managers are left-brained - introverted, practical, controlling organisers. Leaders are right-brained – extrovert, innovative, caring flexibles.

❑ Demonstrate how you can transform your management and leadership of an individual member of staff.

❑ Consider the impact of the move from left-brained to right-brained language (e.g. "control" to "empower") as the new "politically correct" organisational norm.

❑ Resolve the paradox that left-brained managers provide radically different answers from right-brained leaders to the same important strategic questions; e.g Tony Blair "empowered" Gordon Brown. Gordon Brown "controlled" the UK. The question was: "How do we get the best out of those for whom we are responsible?"

❑ Conclude with a compelling argument as to why, since the 1970s, nearly all CEOs have followed a series of Critical Strategic Drivers (CSDs) that have failed to produce sustainable increases in profitability and identify the single driver – the one right answer – that will deliver effective cultural change and a significant, sustainable increase in profitability very rapidly.

MANAGEMENT AND LEADERHIP

MANAGER	LEADER
❑ Left-brained	❑ Right-brained
❑ Closes down	❑ Opens up
Introvert	*Extrovert*
❑ Private and contained	❑ Sociable and expressive
❑ Expresses emotions within themselves	❑ Expresses emotions to TOPs
❑ Learns in a quiet setting with extended mental reflection	❑ Learns through doing and discussing
Practical	*Innovative*
❑ Focuses on what is real and factual	❑ Is imaginative and innovative
❑ Thinks inside the box	❑ Thinks outside the box
❑ Builds carefully and thoroughly towards conclusions	❑ Moves quickly to conclusions following hunches
Controlling	*Caring*
❑ Strives for an objective statement of truth, when rational, and to get their own way, when irrational	❑ Strives for harmony and positive interactions
❑ Challenges and questions	❑ Incorporates diverse viewpoints into compromises that satisfy as many TOPs as possible
❑ Criticises	❑ Is kind and tolerant towards TOPs

MANAGER	LEADER
Organised	*Flexible*
❑ Has things decided	❑ Keeps things loose and open to change
❑ Allows plenty of time to plan and focus to avoid the stress of last minute deadlines	❑ Works with imminent deadlines as they generate most creativity and energy
❑ Is methodical and systematic	❑ Makes decisions on the spur of the moment, "goes with the flow"

MANAGERS

❑ Managers are introverted, practical, controlling organisers. They like to focus inwards and close down. They operate on what is termed the left-side of the brain.

❑ If the "dark" or, from their perspective, "leadership" sides are underdeveloped, then managers:

– Cannot motivate, as human beings do not like being treated as robots.
– Cannot manage change, as for them change is an extrapolation from the past. As President John F. Kennedy said: "In a world of change, those who only live in the past and present are certain to miss the future."

❑ Managers are clearly defined to themselves and TOPS, as there is a reinforcement of beliefs across the dimensions. This is particularly strong across the practical and organising dimension.

❑ Good managers, with no avoidances in the polar opposite dimensions, quoting Peter F. Drucker, "do things right".

LEADERS

❑ Leaders are extroverted, innovative, caring flexibles. They like to focus outwards and open up. They operate on what is termed the right side of the brain.

❑ If the "dark" or, from their perspective, "management" sides are underdeveloped, then leaders:

– Cannot manage change. They live in the future as visionaries but can never "make the dream come true", never translate "vision into action".

– Can inspire TOPs but, at the end of the day, motivation burns out in the absence of any effective action. In extreme cases, leaders can lead themselves and their followers over the edge of a cliff in pursuit of the impossible dream in an impractical way.

❑ Can also demotivate followers by starting off a multitude of hares. The followers become bewildered and exhausted by pursuing a multitude of "dreams" simultaneously.

❑ Leaders are clearly defined to themselves and TOPS, as there is a reinforcement of beliefs across the dimensions. This is particularly strong across the innovative and flexible dimensions.

❑ Good leaders, with no avoidances in the polar opposite dimensions, quoting Peter F. Drucker, "do the right things".

Author's note
I refer to the combination as an M&L – whole-brained. M&Ls: "do the right things right".

MANAGER V LEADER

❑ Tony Blair and Gordon Brown represent a fascinating example of how their combined profile produced a "marriage made in heaven" but ensured ultimate failure because opposites do not attract, and also ensured both went into and stayed in excess – "strength into weakness".

❑ Set out below is the combined M&L profile

Introvert (Gordon)	Extrovert (Tony)
Practical (Gordon)	Innovative (Tony)
Control (Gordon)	Care (Tony)
Organised (Tony)	Flexible (Gordon)

❑ Tony's single management competence in "Organised" made him a more effective leader, as it enabled him to translate "vision into action". Gordon's single leadership competence in "Flexible" made him a less effective manager, as it led to indecisiveness or "dithering".

❑ Together they were complete – a marriage made in heaven. They had the perfect M&L profile. They complemented each other beautifully. However, polar opposites hate each other, unless they have developed understanding, appreciation and competence in the "dark sides" – scores of, at the least, 2.

❑ This did not happen, as there was no incentive for it to happen. There were two reasons:

1. Most people, when they reach the top, stop learning, if they have not stopped somewhere earlier on the ladder to success.
2. Why bother working in areas in which you are not naturally competent and cause you stress to operate in, when someone who is naturally competent will do your "dirty work"?

❑ As a result they hated each other. It was always a marriage of political convenience, which worked very well in delivering three successive election victories. But it was bound to end in tears.

❑ Critically they stayed in their respective areas of natural competence, permanently locked in the comfort and not the learning zone, and they both went into excess.

❑ With Gordon, there was too much control, too much detail, too much introversion and it brought out the worst of the Flexible – indecisiveness

❑ With Tony, it was party, party, party at Downing Street; spin, spin, spin with an obsession on image.

EFFECTIVELY M&L A "DIRECT REPORT"

We look at:

- ❑ Use the four M&L communication styles (CS) appropriately
- ❑ Develop clarity of role.
- ❑ Ensure effective job descriptions.
- ❑ Set standards and performance measures.
- ❑ Give praise.
- ❑ Give constructive criticism.
- ❑ Use appraisals to create learning and growth.

USE THE FOUR M&L COMMUNICATION STYLES (CS) APPROPRIATELY

These are:

CS1 = Tell
CS2 = Coach
CS3 = Support
CS4 = Delegate

Looking at each in turn:

CS1 = Tell

There are three occasions, when we, as the M&L, should use the CS1 "tell" style:

- ❑ A crisis.
- ❑ A member of our staff is new to the job.
- ❑ There is sudden change, perceived negatively.

A crisis

- ❑ If there is a crisis, then it is our role to resolve it. Imagine the Captain of the Titanic, when the iceberg had struck, calling all his officers together and saying: "Gentlemen, we have a problem. An iceberg has just struck us. So let us pour ourselves a stiff drink, eh, and have a chin-wag – a brainstorm to promote discovery of the various options, and then spend some time action planning. With, of course, a full review of the plan, before implementing it. It's 3 p.m., and if we get started now, we should be ready for effective action in 4 hours!"

❑ Of course not. As leaders, we seize control and tell our followers what to do, why and how, so that the crisis is rapidly resolved. I would emphasise that we do not simply tell people what to do, as some M&Ls do, we must also give a clear explanation of the crisis or reason requiring the action we suggest. Nor is covering "what" and "why" sufficient. We must give clear guidance on the specifics of the "how".

❑ "Gentlemen, we have been hit by an iceberg. We must abandon ship immediately with a minimum of panic. Harry, you will be responsible for conveying the news to the passengers and organising their move to the life-boats; George you will be responsible for getting the passengers onto the life-boats and lowering them to the sea, applying the principle of women and children first; Charles, you will send out distress signals; Matthew will......and so on. The sequence I propose is....

❑ Any questions, ladies and gentlemen? No......... Then proceed to action."

Member of staff new to the job
Where a member of staff (who has just joined or changed roles) is new to a job, and likely to lack confidence and be feeling insecure, then we need to "tell" in a constructive way – provide clear guidance on "what" needs to be done, "why" and "how" and monitor performance. We would also provide a measure of support by having an open door policy, if they run into difficulties.

Sudden negative change
We will look at this in more detail in Chapter 9, "Create Growth from Change". Sudden change, perceived negatively, can cause a loss of self-esteem, uncertainty and negative emotions. The M&L needs to take control of the situation to avoid the team splitting at the seams or the individual becoming demotivated and incompetent.

CS2 – Coaching

This style is used where a staff member has gained a degree of competence and confidence. We still provide the "what" and the "why", but involve the staff member in the "how", seek his or her input, and listen to the views expressed – so there is a genuine dialogue about and agreement to the implementation. We should also make ourselves available, if they run into difficulties.

CS3 – Supporting

This is used when we now have a confident and competent member of staff, who can do the job well. So we advise them what they need to do and why, but trust them to determine for themselves the "how". We remain in touch by having an open door policy and being available to support, if there are problems/unexpected difficulties encountered by our member of staff.

CS4 – Delegating

A style, especially used at higher levels in an organisation, when the leader expects her or his lieutenants to be able to run the part of the organisation for which they are responsible and provides little direction or support. Without the use of the earlier styles, as appropriate, this style is known as "dumping".

Key Points

❑ The progression through the four M&L communication styles can be viewed as an effective process of delegation – from control to empowerment.

❑ There is a need to avoid developing a mindset based on false assumptions. We illustrate this point with the case study entitled, "the falling star".

The Falling Star

I talked to a partner in a City Law Firm about one of his senior associates, who was coming on a development programme. The partner was extremely enthusiastic. *"He is a star. He is on the fast track to partnership and he deserves it. He is no trouble at all.*

Any work I give to him, he does to a very high standard and always by the deadline, which can be very short, as some of our clients are very demanding indeed.

I don't have to spend any time with him and never have to go through his drafts with him to point out all his mistakes. This is not the case with all my other associates, which is why he is a star, as he knows and all his colleagues know."

I then talked to the senior associate, and discovered one of the unhappiest individuals I had ever met.

Paraphrasing his words. *"I am at my wit's end. I get no support or praise from my partner – I hardly ever see him. He just dumps work on me and lets me get on with it.*

I am very isolated, as all my peers know I am on the fast track to partnership and so I have lost the few friends I had. What is even worse is that I get given assignments to complete that require a technical skill level I lack when I get them. I have no one to turn to for help.

My partner is always going on about his other associates asking him stupid questions and I simply cannot admit ignorance to him.

I wouldn't be his bloody little star if I did. I cannot consult any of my colleagues, as they resent me because I am going to make partner ahead of them.

Well what do I do? Well I start going mad. I am already doing 2,400 chargeable hours, with my target set at 1,600, as I get lumbered with all the high profile deals my partner cannot handle.

On top of that I have to spend hours and hours at night (when I am not doing an all-nighter on a deal) looking up all the precedents and studying all the know-how documents to get the answers to the technical areas I don't understand. I have no friends, no partner, no sex life, and no time for myself – nothing except work, work, work and more work."

❑ The lesson for the M&L is to always ask the member of staff whether there are any aspects of the job being delegated where they might need additional guidance or training to help them succeed.

❑ If we recognise the level of confidence and ability of our members of staff, and the nature of the situation they face, we can then choose the communication style that is appropriate. By doing this we develop a flexible and appropriate response – effective M&Ls in this critical area.

Author's notes

❑ I made the suggestion that until the follower is fully competent, you should adopt an open door policy, e.g. "If you run into any difficulties, I am here to help – don't hesitate to come to see me."

❑ A manager, when we were discussing this, said that that was not a good idea. From her experience, it was far better to say that, if they ran into any difficulties, they should do some research and see if they could come up with some suggested solutions themselves and then she would be delighted to have a chat to agree what was the best way forward, i.e. "bring me solutions not problems."

❑ I think this is a very sound suggestion, as otherwise you are keeping them in a parent/child relationship rather than encouraging them to think for themselves as adults. It is a way of accelerating their path to flying "solo".

DEVELOP CLARITY OF ROLE

❑ I have met many, many managers, where lack of clarity in their role has caused enormous stress. They find that they are doing work they should not be doing, duplicating other's work or having someone else doing part of the job, for which they are responsible and accountable.

❑ One particular case that sticks in my mind was an individual who had been hired to be the Marketing Director, when his predecessor had been appointed Managing Director. The Managing Director, for understandable reasons in terms of staying within his comfort zone, made the Marketing Director's life a complete misery by giving endless unsolicited advice and keeping under his direct control those aspects of his former role, which he enjoyed.

❑ If you are responsible for a team of managers or employees, the best approach to this problem is to agree collectively the individual role.

ENSURE EFFECTIVE JOB DESCRIPTIONS

❑ Job descriptions tend not to be helpful, as they often list many qualities that cannot easily be assessed, have a lot of detail about role and responsibilities rather than key areas for action and actions required, and occasionally ask for attributes that are mutually exclusive, e.g. must be a decisive leader and a team player.

❑ The best way to develop an action oriented job description is to use a top-down thinking approach. By way of example, we have:

Situation
Jo is appointed to a new role.

Complication
Jo is not clear about her role.

Key Question
What should Jo do?

Answer or Governing Strategic Action (GSA)
Agree an action-oriented job description with her M&L.

Key Question that Naturally Comes into the Reader's Mind
What are the drivers for strategic action?

Provide the Answers at the Keyline – The Action Drivers

1. Delight her clients.
2. Generate new business.

3. Build an effective team.
4. M&L her staff.

Ask the Question that Naturally Comes into the Reader's Mind for Each Action Area and Answer it
Looking at the first action driver by way of example, we have:

1. Delight her clients (how?)

   – Agree needs.
   – Meet needs.
   – Provide after sales care.
   – Develop long-term partnership.

This would lead to lower level "hows", e.g.

Agree needs

   – Understand business/cultural context.
   – Develop empathy.
   – Ensure own expertise recognized.
   – Develop thinking.
   – Demonstrate value to be added.
   – Agree standards.

❑ At the end of this process, each jobholder has a precise idea of specific actions required to carry out their role successfully. It gives a template for effective time management. Any activity in the list is important and worth spending time on and any activity that is not part of her revised job description is unimportant and worth spending little or no time at all on.

AGREE STANDARDS AND PERFORMANCE MEASURES
We start with a case study, "Ignorance is not bliss".

Ignorance is not bliss

A manager, Julie, attended a two module development programme. We had looked at the need to praise when a direct report had met a standard for the first time (praising is covered in the next section).

Julie mentioned that she had a direct report who was very competent, but she could never praise him, as her standards were so high. I asked her to provide an example.

She did. She said that she had developed a very effective project management methodology and her direct report simply had not managed his projects to her standard. I then innocently asked her if she had advised her direct report of this very effective methodology. Julie said "no".

The start of the second module was a review of the personal development plan formed at the end of the first module and implemented before the second. Julie was delighted to advise that her direct report had now met all her high standards, had been praised regularly and their working relationship had been transformed.

❑ Performance cannot be measured unless there are standards agreed against which performance can be benchmarked. There will be many generic standards such as timeliness, behavioural standards, and dress standards as well as work standards. If any have not been set (and agreed at the time of the job interview), then you, like Julie, need to set them initially.

❑ This can be done through the delegation process already covered. Initially, you use the CS1 "tell" communication style, detailing the "how" when you set the standards. As your direct report gets more confident, you share the "how" under the CS2 "coaching" style, i.e. agree standards. With CS3 "Supporting" or CS4 "Delegating", they are setting their own standards, as you now trust them completely. They have been empowered.

❑ These performance measures are concerned with how the jobholder carries out his role on a day-to-day basis. The other performance measures are the S.M.A.R.T objectives to be agreed in all the key action areas.

- Specific
- Measurable
- Agreed
- Realistic
- Timed

❏ I mention the need to set them in all key action areas, as many organisations focus purely on hard business objectives, e.g. the senior associate who had to achieve 1600 billable hours in a law firm or the consultant who has to achieve 70% profitable utilisation or the salesperson who has to sell £300,000 worth of business.

❏ Our behaviour tends to follow our reward systems. Reward systems tend to focus on hard business measures. So we tend to focus all our energies on achieving these hard targets on which promotion and/or bonuses depend. The fact that we do our jobs the best, perform the best and get the best results if we focus on all the key action areas is lost on us and the organisations we serve.

❏ We can always create useful qualitative measures of success in any key action area. For instance, if we have to delight internal or external clients, we can carry out customer satisfaction surveys with an overall satisfaction rating. If that were to come out first time at 70%, then we can set a S.M.A.R.T objective. "Within one year, the overall satisfaction rating will have moved from 70% to 90% (and we can also set interim milestones if we want to measure progress)."

GIVE PRAISE

❏ Giving praise in the right way for the right reason at the right time is generally an underdeveloped and under-utilised skill. Too often we forget to praise, as we are too busy ourselves or we operate in cultures where criticism is the cultural norm. Too often we praise in vague and unhelpful ways, e.g. "You're a star." Too often we praise before dumping!

❏ Here we look at the three key questions:

- Why praise?

– When to praise?
– How to praise?

Why Praise?

The fundamental reason for giving praise is to acknowledge good performance and so encourage the continuance of that good performance. When done effectively, it takes less than a minute and is time very well spent.

When to Praise?

There are three occasions when praise should be given. When:

1. Work meets an agreed standard for the first time.
2. Work exceeds an agreed standard.
3. Work is satisfactory over a long period of time.

1. Work meets an agreed standard for the first time

As you know, standards are set when someone is new to the role and when you first delegate using the CS1 "Tell" style. By making the time, in the first instance, to:

❑ Advise the "what".
❑ Advise the "why".
❑ Provide the "detailed" how and set the standards for the specific job being delegated.
❑ Confirm understanding through an open question.
❑ Confirm availability and the "bring me solutions" suggestion.

You are guaranteeing that your direct report will meet the standards for the first time and so can be given praise. This starts the relationship off on a virtuous circle where mutual respect is created.

Author's note

❑ We often finish briefing by asking the closed question, "do you understand?" The direct report inevitably says "yes" as you are the "boss" and they do not want to ask "stupid questions".

❑ It is excellent practice to ask them to recap what you have said so that any misunderstandings, misperceptions or confusions are cleared up before, rather than after they go away to do the job.

2. Work exceeds an agreed standard
By praising those that outperform – the stars – it encourages them to continue.

3. Work is satisfactory over a long period of time
For every star there are solid performers, often supporting the stars, who keep the required standards over a long period of time. They can become neglected and feel unloved – so praising them occasionally, but regularly, pays enormous dividends.

How to Give Praise?

❑ A time sequence of activities with an example is provided below:

– Start by scoping the performance you want to praise.

"Anne, I'd like to talk to you about the report you've prepared over the past three weeks..."

– Quote a specific example (or examples) of the individual's performance.

"I'm impressed with the fact that you placed the recommendations at the front of the report so I could see immediately the decisions we need to take..."

– Mention personal qualities.

"I also noticed that you've put in a lot of extra hours to meet the deadline and that you were persistent in getting information from managers who weren't particularly forthcoming..."

   – Comment on how this benefits the achievement of the team's overall objectives.

"The report is going to be used as part of our decision-making at the executive meeting next week.

   – Conclude.

"Thank you very much for your sterling efforts. I appreciate them."

❑   This is short, to the point, and highlights the specific qualities and skills you want to be maintained. Moreover, by providing the necessary detail to praise for good performance, you are showing interest in the direct report, which is also highly motivational. Those M&Ls, who praise on the, "you're a star" basis, don't realise that the lack of specifics means that they have not observed and are not showing real interest. This form of praise, especially if repetitive, demotivates.

❑   Before moving on to constructive criticism, how we receive praise affects whether we get praise in the future. Those who say, "it was nothing" or, "it was mainly someone else" will find they will not get much praise again. The simplest way to receive praise is to say, "Thank you".

GIVE CONSTRUCTIVE CRITICISM

❑   When we receive criticism where the "intention" is to be constructive, the manifestation of that intention or the environment in which the intention is manifested means that we feel simply criticised, which impacts on our self-esteem and makes us angry and defensive.

❑   I do not know of anyone who goes home with a song in their heart and a smile on their faces to say to their loved ones: *"It has been a fantastic day today. I have received masses and masses of constructive criticism"* or using the now "politically correct" terminology: *"It has been a fantastic day today. I have received masses and masses of development opportunities. I am slightly concerned that, as I have so many development opportunities, I may be "let go" to fulfil the enormous potential that I clearly have."*

❏ Before we give constructive criticism, we should recognise five things.

1. Art critics can give rave reviews – so we should mention the positives as well as the negatives.
2. The time is when performance has dropped below an agreed standard (and not "out of the blue" at the annual appraisal).
3. The sole objective is to raise the performance back to that standard – so we need to have calmed down and got into a positive frame of mind before the discussion.
4. We need to do it in a way that does not erode self-esteem or confidence.
5. We need to recognise that the way we have performed as their M&L may have contributed to the member of staff's poor performance and be prepared to acknowledge that reality.

I set out a suggested process with an example:

– Start by scoping the performance you need to criticise.

"Anne I need to talk to you about your handling of the meeting this morning..."

– Praise any good aspects of the performance.

"You kept a really tight rein on the meeting and ensured that everything on the agenda was covered..."

– Specify your concerns.

"One area that concerned me was the lack of contribution from some of the quieter members of the team..."

– Ask for suggestions.

"If you had to run that meeting again what could you do to make sure you get more input from the quieter members....?"

– Make your own suggestions.

This may or may not be necessary depending on the response to the previous question. There may be an opportunity to build on an idea, which has been suggested in their response.

– Agree on the action to be taken.

"OK, so at next week's meeting you'll allow more time for people to respond and if necessary ask people directly for a contribution......."

– follow-up.

"Let's have a brief chat after next week's meeting and see how you feel it's gone."

Key points

❏ After the praise, do not add a "but" or a "however", as, when we do that, the person knows that criticism is round the corner and all the preceding positives are instantly erased from memory.

❏ Notice the use of the word "concern" which is a nice euphemism for "criticism".

❏ The use of the first person "me" is effectively assertive.

❏ Bring all the evidence of the poor performance with you, just in case there is denial.

❏ Moving straight into "ask for suggestions" is a very powerful approach for 2 reasons.

1. It avoids rubbing their noses in their poor performance. Most managers, or staff, I have met, know when they have done something badly, are kicking themselves and are keen to improve.

2. This is a "coaching" question. People are much more likely to

commit to actions they have put forward or discovered for themselves than to those imposed (suggested) by the M&L.

USE APPRAISALS TO CREATE LEARNING AND GROWTH

☐ The annual appraisal (better termed "performance review") meeting should contain no surprises, as there should be regular reviews of performance either quarterly or when a major project has been completed.

☐ Its focus should be on producing a development plan for the coming year so that performance, growth and learning are maximised.

☐ To ensure that any performance review achieves its objectives, the two principles to be adopted are "leadership by example" and "promoting discovery" (or coaching).

Agree Objective

"As you know, the objective of this meeting is to review your performance and agree a development plan that will result in improved performance....

Lead by Example

"However, to start with, as I am your line manager, I would like us to agree where I have made positive contributions to your performance as well as areas where I personally could have managed better".

Start with the positive

Where I feel I have had a positive impact are in the areas of......
Examples I can provide are.........
What do you think?...

Follow with the negative

Where I feel I could have been more effective is the area of......
Examples are...
What do think?...

Commit to action

I think that to be a better M&L this year, I need to commit to.........

Promote Discovery
Start with the positive
Now, over to you Chris.
Where do you think you performed well this year?
What examples can you provide?
What we do to ensure that next year you spend more time playing to your strengths and improving those areas of excellence?

Follow with the negative
Turning now to development areas, what are the areas where you would like support?
What examples can you provide?

Commit to joint action
What specifically should you do to ensure an improvement in the areas we have agreed?
How can I help you achieve success?

WHAT IS POLITICALLY CORRECT?

- ❑ We now look simultaneously at:
- ❑ The impact of the move from left-brained to right-brained language as the new "politically correct" organisational norm.
- ❑ How to resolve the paradox that left-brained managers provide radically different answers from right-brained leaders to the same important strategic questions.
- ❑ We achieve this by considering the table on the next page entitled: "What is politically correct?" which contains the key questions and the opposing answers given by left-brained managers as compared to right-brained leaders.

QUESTION	LEFT-BRAINED MANAGEMENT ANSWER OR "SPEAK"	RIGHT-BRAINED LEADERSHIP ANSWER OR "SPEAK"
How do we determine the future?	Produce a mission	Create a vision
How do we M&L our staff?	Control them	Empower them
How do we enable them to develop?	Tell them Send them as delegates on training programmes	Coach them Encourage them to fulfill their potential by being participants on development programmes?
How do we view our staff?	Staff are our greatest asset Working at the coal-face Working at the front-line	Internal clients Delight our clients
Who represents the interests of staff?	Human resources Department Personnel Department	and Learning
What do we call our staff?	Our subordinates	Team-members

QUESTION	LEFT-BRAINED MANAGEMENT ANSWER OR "SPEAK"	RIGHT-BRAINED LEADERSHIP ANSWER OR "SPEAK"
What happens when staff are surplus to requirements?	Fired Sacked Made redundant Downsized Restructured	"Let go" to pursue their career interests elsewhere or spend time with their families (assuming they have one)
What do our staff call us?	The boss	N/A

KEY POINT

I think that the general principle is that you should use, where employees are concerned, the right-brained language that acknowledges that they are human beings rather than the left-brained language that considers them robots. We now look at each question in the same order.

HOW DO WE DETERMINE THE FUTURE?

☐ In the 1960s, it was all "mission" e.g. "mission impossible". Now it is all "vision" – the language of change. Both are required. A vision inspires, a mission enables the vision to be implemented. John F Kennedy's statement: "In 10 years, we will have landed a man on the moon" was a mission.

☐ It was successful because there was sufficient visionary language in the rest of his speeches to motivate. Indeed, at the time of the mission statement, the technologies were not in place to fulfil the mission. The other motivational factor was the highly competitive race to be first, ahead of the then Soviet Union.

☐ It gave a time-frame to implement the vision – make the dream come true. Of course, once the mission is in place, then you have to develop the strategic action plan with all the interim milestones.

☐ Martin Luther King's speech, "I have a dream", used highly visionary and motivational language and painted a picture of racial harmony and equality. There was no mission and hence no strategic action plan, as the vision was not adopted by the white decision-takers.

❑ What is often neglected is to produce a picture of the vision as a "picture paints a thousand words". The power of a picture is illustrated by the case study, entitled "Pepsi".

Pepsi

For around 4 years, we finished the first module of the Senior Executive Development programme with a morning session entitled, "vision into action".

After some input and discussion, the groups went off to their syndicate rooms to develop one of the team-member's "vision" and then produce the "vision into action". They then presented back in plenary.

Now I must have listened to hundreds of such presentations. I can only remember one. I would imagine it was the only one that was successful "back at the ranch". It was the "vision into action" of the Marketing Director of Pepsi Cola in the UK.

At that time (around 1995), Coca Cola dominated the high street – had a virtual monopoly in all the retails outlets in the high streets.

The marketing director's presentation was short and sweet. His group had drawn a typical high street. In the middle, dwarfing all the houses, sat a giant can of Pepsi (the vision) and underneath was the mission: "Within 3 years we will dominate the high street". As already mentioned, he was successful.

HOW DO WE VIEW OUR STAFF?

❑ You still read in Reports and Accounts that, "staff are our greatest asset". It is an interesting example of the power of SPO. Once you start thinking of "Reports and Accounts", you inevitably fall into accountant "mindset" – where the word "asset" rules OK. I suppose that, with significant downsizing for a given company, we will read that, "staff are our wasted asset" – how true for how many companies.

❑ Coal-face has rather unpleasant historic connotations. "Front-line" implies a battle with the hated enemy – not quite the right message to give when trying to "delight" the customers or clients.

HOW DO WE M&L OUR STAFF?

❑ Once you recognise that a "How" question can be answered by a process, i.e. a set of activities in a time order, then the reality emerges that both "control" and "empowerment" are necessary as part of the process to develop a member of staff.

❑ "Tell" and "coach" are part of the same process.

WHO REPRESENTS THE INTERESTS OF STAFF?

❑ Human Resources (HR) and Personnel still prevail, although it is increasingly "Director of HR and Learning".

❑ I favour the current trend where Personnel Departments' non-core processing functions are outsourced and the core role becomes Director of Learning and Development, operating at Board Level. The Finance Director is always there. There are only a few Directors of Learning and Development around and only a few HR Directors operate at Board Level.

❑ One day, CEOs and Chairmen will wake up to the fact that motivating and developing staff is more important to short and long term profitability than the management of money.

WHAT HAPPENS WHEN STAFF ARE SURPLUS TO REQUIREMENTS?

❑ This is the exception to the rule. In my view, in this instance, you should call a "spade" a "spade". You have been "made redundant". The right-brained language sounds and is so false.

❑ I have never heard any individual using that language (apart from politically correct public announcements). Just imagine it. One partner comes home to the other partner and says: "I have chosen to stop earning any filthy lucre so that I can spend more time with you" or "I have chosen not to earn any money for some considerable time, as I need to fulfil my potential by getting a lower paid job in exactly the same line of work, if I can get one."

WHAT DO OUR STAFF CALL US?

❑ Every single individual I have met, whatever their national, cultural or ethnic background refers to their "boss" as their "boss". It is lodged deep in their subconscious, as an incredibly strong mindset.

❑ It derives, of course, from the historic social convention or collective mindset that fathers are "Kings of the Castle" at home, directly transported to "paternalistic" cultures at work. Critically important, of course, is that most fathers in the past (and still in the present in some sub-cultures) behaved as the "Boss" at home. In many countries round the world, of course, the societal norm and "boss behaviour" still prevails.

❑ Recent research, reported in the Times newspaper, revealed that over 85% of parents hit their children in the privacy of their own homes. Of course, women now are encouraged to have exactly the same rights as men. The "I,I,I" culture means that controlling women no longer have societal pressure to develop their caring side. I doubt, therefore, that the percentage will reduce over time – just an effective implementation of the "Equal Opportunities Act".

❑ "Why did you hit me – Daddy/Mummy or Mummy or Mummy/Mummy or Daddy or Daddy/ Daddy"? "Don't ask stupid questions. It is for your own good".

❑ This is why "subordinates" or "team-members" put up with the incredibly bad behaviour many bosses display to them. Driven from the subconscious, they accept behaviour that should not be tolerated, because their psychological resistance is permanently poor.

❑ It is accepted as a childhood norm that the boss has the right to, "*tell you what to do, especially in an arrogant or domineering manner*".

❑ Until I discovered SPO, I had been rather sceptical about the removal of "golly-wogs" and the elimination of the word "nigger" from all literature accessible by children.

❏ Now I know the awesome power of SPO, it was a highly necessary step to take.

❏ "Boss" should be eliminated from the vocabulary and replaced by the innocuous "M&L".

❏ "What's your M&L like?" "A bit heavy on the management and not enough leadership".

FOLLOW THE RIGHT CRITICAL STRATEGIC DRIVER (CSD)

❏ Since the 1970s, companies have failed to maximise their profitability, as they have focussed on a series of Critical Strategic Drivers (CSDs) that simply did not deliver, as set out in the table below.

Critical Strategic Driver (CSD)	Reasons for failure to deliver
Maximise earnings	❏ Pursuing unprofitable projects to meet total income targets. ❏ The perceived means, i.e. the customer, to the desired end was neglected.
Maximise added value to share-holders	❏ IT systems could not measure the profitability of individual projects. Total income targets continued to be set. ❏ The perceived means, i.e. the customer, to the desired end was neglected.
Delight the client	❏ Employees, working in less than delightful environments, failed to delight the client. ❏ The explicit statement, "The customer is king" lead to the implicit belief that staff were "peasants."

CRITICAL STRATEGIC DRIVER (CSD)	REASONS FOR FAILURE TO DELIVER
	❑ The explicit statement, "Client first" lead to the implicit belief that staff came second or were second rate.
Change culture	❑ No ownership by the CMDU (Core Decision-Making Unit) ❑ A separate "vision and values" exercise, thus denying the necessary integration into the fabric of the daily work experience. ❑ Staff demotivated as their role models neither preached nor practiced – or preached but did not practise the values they, the staff, were supposed to follow.
Change for change's sake	❑ Change weariness as the result of frequent 'change management projects' – restructuring, delayering, downsizing and so on. ❑ Demotivation of staff by having to re-apply for their existing jobs with inferior conditions or apply for new jobs that were more onerous or less well paid, assuming they were not "let go".

❑ There is only one right CSD – to deliver effective team-working throughout the company ASAP. This CSD focuses on the true means – the staff - and delivers maximum profitability at minimal cost.

❑ Staff will operate in highly motivational, high performance work environments or cultures.

❑ The team is the best vehicle by far to manage change successfully.

❑ Staff will focus on the client and indeed "delight the client".

❑ The delighted clients will provide, through repeat business, extensions and referrals (with zero marketing costs), the outstanding profitability that has been the goal, but unachievable reality, down the decades for all but a few CEOs.

❑ The next three chapters enable you to learn how to build any group of staff into a high-performing team in 4 hours and how to ensure high performance is maintained. In the final chapter, "Transform Your Company's Profitability", you will learn how any company, whatever its size can have "delivered effective team-working throughout the company" within 6 months of the commencement of a project, I call, "Project Omega".

Chapter 8
Build an Effective Team Very Rapidly

INTRODUCTION

❑ I have developed a unique recipe - a set of tools, techniques and processes - that creates an effective team in four hours. It has been successfully applied to over a 1000 groups of employees from PAs and night-shift print workers to CMDUs – Core Decision-Making Units. Many of the groups have had up to 4 different staff levels represented and many have included very culturally diverse individuals.

"Rupert's principles and approach worked every time across job levels and national cultures. When his techniques have been practised sufficiently to become habitual, they result in huge leaps forward in creativity and decision-making. They also refresh the parts other approaches cannot reach, building strength and confidence for both the team and the individual. Creating and being part of a great team produces better results, makes work more rewarding and helps people to grow. Good managers want this for themselves and those who work with them. Rupert provides all the guidance needed to turn aspiration into reality". Martin Pexton: Personnel Director of Allen & Overy (a global city law firm) from 1990-2002; Corporate Development Director of London Merchant Securities from 2002-2007 and Managing Director LMS Capital from 2007-2009.

❑ This chapter transfers the recipe to you, the reader, and enables you to build any group, for which you are or become responsible, whether as manager of a number of direct reports or team-leader of a newly formed project group, into a high-performing team in 4 hours. The workshop can take place on site in a meeting room.

❑ I start this chapter by setting out the results of building a high performing team, consider the benefits that you will enjoy, then set out, in detail, what is the preparation required before you run your in-house workshop, the four steps involved, and conclude with a summary, entitled "Recipe for Action".

THE RESULTS

The results of building your group(s) into a winning team in the workplace are:

❑ The output and effectiveness of a high-performing team is always greater than the sum of its individual parts – what is termed, "synergy". *"You will get better results faster than before"*, as Martin mentioned above.

❑ As part of the process of creating your winning team, you will produce an action plan to progress your most important strategic issue. Your team-members will be highly motivated to ensure rapid and successful implementation of that plan. When we operate in an environment where our work is more rewarding than before, and we are growing as individuals, we become highly motivated and driven to create success for our team-mates, as well as ourselves.

❑ As a result, your team-members will become a great support to each other and to you.

THE BENEFITS FOR YOU

The benefits for you are that:

❑ Your career prospects will be enhanced. Bosses tend to reward direct reports who produce outstanding performance for them, as they can, rightly, shine in reflected glory.

❑ Office politics will be minimised within your area of control.

❑ The work environment or local culture will be very positive –

everyone will have high job satisfaction and energy levels.
- ❏ Your quality of working life will improve.
- ❏ You will be able to achieve, what has hitherto been extremely elusive for most, a real work-life balance.

PREPARE

Before you take the first step, there are 5 pieces of information you need to know/ actions to take:

- ❏ Recognise the limitation in group size
- ❏ Act as a co-ordinator
- ❏ Believe in yourself
- ❏ Believe in your group members
- ❏ Prepare for your workshop

1. RECOGNISE THE LIMITATION IN GROUP SIZE

- ❏ You may have noticed that I have frequently referred in the previous chapters to the word "group" rather than "team". This is deliberate. Many years ago, I was talking to the Managing Director of a multi-national travel services company. During the course of the conversation, he said to me: "I have a fantastic team". So, I said to him: "That's great, and how many are in your team?" To which he replied, "ten thousand" (the entire work-force).
- ❏ The point is that, if you want to create an effective team, there is a limitation on the numbers (including yourself) that comprise the unit. Of the 1000 groups I mentioned, the smallest group size was four and the largest group size was seven.
- ❏ The reason why we have a cut-off of four is that you need a critical mass of group members to produce the benefits of effective group working.
- ❏ The reason for the cut-off of seven is because of what happens when you are part of an effective team. It is a wonderful, exhilarating and rewarding experience. Without consciously recognising it, your ego becomes suppressed as your needs are being met by the power of the group.

❑ Your focus becomes external rather than internal. You become very aware of other group members and want to help them. There is a limit to how many people we can become aware of at the same time. Again that that is true is not in doubt. We look at the first case study – learning from my mistakes.

Learning from my mistakes

This is the answer given to me by the Managing Partner of an international office of a Global Law Firm to the following question: "What had been the most recent challenges he had faced and what had he learnt from them?"

"Well, funny you should ask that as I have just finished being the lead partner in a big multimillion dollar, multi-jurisdictional transaction that lasted 9 months and involved 25 lawyers from a number of different offices working full-time. It was successful but it was a nightmare with enormous stress and 'blood on the carpet' on the way. I made two key mistakes.

First of all, I spent far too much time thinking and planning this vital transaction on my own. This meant that, when I called in the other partners, I controlled far too much and I pushed through decisions that backfired. I should have been an effective co-ordinator rather than an ineffective controller.

Secondly, we got all 25 lawyers together for a day. God that was awful – incredible heat and very little light. In hindsight, I should have started with a project steering group with me as co-ordinator and four other senior partners. Each of the partners should have been the co-ordinator of a sub-group of around 4 or 5 lawyers. Then we should have had a team-based strategic planning day, which would have created an effective strategy and action plans and the momentum to drive them through."

2. ACT AS A CO-ORDINATOR.

❑ Over two years ago, I had some fascinating confirmation of both the need to act as a co-ordinator and keep the team size between

4 and 7. I listened to Paul Azinger, in a TV interview, explain why the US won the Ryder Cup in 2008.

❑ The US were significant underdogs as they had lost the four previous encounters. The UK team was lead by Nick Faldo, a strange choice in that he was noted as a being a self-centred individualistic type of person – but then the UK is not big on teams, as covered in the introduction.

❑ What Paul Azinger did was to split the 12 players into 3 pods of four. He had 3 lieutenants, as compared to Nick Faldo's one, for which he was criticised as showing weak leadership. He said that he thought it had showed strong leadership as he trusted them, they had clear roles and they got on well with the players.

❑ Paul Azinger also said that he picked the pairings on the basis of like personalities rather than like games, i.e. people who got on well with each other rather than people who played golf in a similar way.

❑ In short, a handsome victory was achieved, reversing the underdog status because:

1. Paul was a co-ordinator of his team rather than a "command and control" leader with no team.

2. His lieutenants' key role was also co-ordinating/coaching – helping to build each of the 3 pods into high-performing units, in which they were successful.

❑ So the team approach enabled the US to exceed all expectations, as the American golfers played, "out of their skins". The individualistic approach meant that the European golfers fell below what was expected of them, given their overall superior position in the individual rankings. Too many did not: "step up to the plate".

❑ It is, of course, the same in any sport with large team numbers. You can have team spirit in rugby, football and cricket (taking but three examples), but, to have effective team-working, you need to break the team down into units, e.g. defensive/midfield/attacking for football and not try the impossible, i.e. to create effective team-working from the full group rather than the smaller units.

❏ Finishing on a footballing note, when the attacking unit has become an effective team, then all the individuals focus on maximising the probability that a shot on goal will produce a goal. Hence the brilliant passing to the player who can "tap in" rather than endless low probability scoring shots by players, ignoring the unmarked player screaming for the pass, concentrating on individual glory (and to be fair, sometimes, job survival) at the expense of team success.

Author's notes

❏ We have just won the Ashes in a fantastic 3-1 defeat of the Aussies (I am typing this note on 7th January 2011, having watched the triumph unwind until the early hours). In fact, it is the first time in history that the Aussies have been beaten in their own backyard 3 times by an innings and a number of runs.

❏ All the English cricketers, without exception, highlighted the wonderful team spirit in the dressing room. All the top performers, without exception, down-played their own individual performance and praised their colleagues.

❏ All the commentators and Jimmy Anderson himself pointed out that the bowlers had performed as a unit and that Jimmy Anderson (who had taken more wickets in an Ashes series in Australia than any other English bowler since Frank "Typhoon" Tyson in 1954-55) had been the "leader of the pack". He had, without any formal training, become an effective co-ordinator of the group of bowlers.

❏ In the Ashes 5-0 drubbing or "whitewash" by the Aussies in 2005, we had an excess of individualism with Andrew Flintoff and a very large ego trying to "lead from the front". Jimmy Anderson was a disaster.

❏ One of the key strengths of Andrew Strauss, as captain, was to treat his players as adults and give them responsibility. I was fascinated by a short interview that started with Michael Atherton talking to Graeme Swann and Kevin Pietersen. Andrew Strauss wandered into the group, clutching the sacred urn. Atherton asked the two what they thought of their leader.

❑   Instantly, in a jocular but very meaningful manner, Swann replied, and I cannot recall the exact words, "the single fact that he gave the bowlers responsibility to set their field placings". Strauss had delegated to the experts – a very smart move.

❑   In contrast, all the bowlers in the Aussie side were treated as individuals, accountable to their batting captain. There was a very revealing moment in the final test. Halfway through a Johnson over, when he was spraying the ball all over the pitch, his captain (Michael Clarke for this final test) instructed him from the slips to switch to bowling "around the wicket".

❑   Can you imagine it? Here is a bowler, who, if he had bowled in a team environment, would have been the number 1 bowler in the world, being "told off" like a naughty school boy, in front of all his peers, to change his behaviour. I imagine he could not help himself. He disobeyed and bowled the next three balls "over the wicket".

❑   The next over he bowled was "around the wicket".

❑   The received wisdom, before the start of battle, was that the sides were very evenly matched. It was Strauss and Andy Flower, the coach, generating a work ethic (endless practice harnessing the power of SPO and substantially increasing individual skill levels), Strauss developing a fantastic team spirit, and "empowering" the bowlers to bowl as an effective unit (and also the batsmen, as they were highly supportive of each other) that produced the thumping victory.

3. BELIEVE IN YOURSELF

❑   You will be the only one of your team to have read this book. Knowledge gives you power and increases self-belief. The very act of reading this and the next two chapters – developing your awareness and understanding – will increase your confidence.

❑   You can also practise any of the tools and techniques, covered in the main body of the book that you deem helpful, to ensure that you are totally confident, before the big day, that you will be successful.

4. BELIEVE IN YOUR GROUP MEMBERS

❑ In a research experiment into the impact of expectations on results, around 60 young school children of average ability were split into three equal groups. Each group was taught by a different teacher, none of whom had met the children before. Let us call the teachers A, B and C. The A teacher was told that she was receiving bright, able, committed children; the B teacher was told that she was receiving average, run-of-the-mill kids and the C teacher was told that she was getting a bunch of below average, rude and rebellious children – the "dross".

❑ Six months later, all the children in each of the three groups were performing and behaving exactly according to the expectations given to each teacher.

❑ If you have faith in the potential of all your group members, suspend your initial judgements formed from working with them on an individual basis and rigorously avoid the display of any favouritism, each group member will have confidence in themselves, derived from the confidence you show in them and you will be able to create a high-performing team.

5. PREPARE FOR THE WORKSHOP

❑ You need to get a date in diaries for an on-site half-day for all the team-members. All they need to know is that the objective of the half-day is to improve team-working, which could, of course, be very good to start with. You will need a separate meeting room with table and chairs, one flip-chart, plenty of flip-chart pens and spare flip-chart paper.

❑ You will also need blue tack or masking tape to hang your output around the walls. There should be no individual pieces of paper or individual writing, apart from you as the co-ordinator or any designated scribe during the actual event.

❑ There will be some material you will want to write up on the flip-chart in advance or hand-out. This will be clearly indicated in the summary plan at the end of this chapter. Coffee, tea and so on should be on tap and, built into the process plan, is a fifteen minute break.

❑ All mobiles should be turned off and there should be no external interruptions. It is absolutely essential that the entire group are together (body and soul) throughout the half day – apart from the official break.

❑ If you don't think your culture permits that, then I would recommend going off-site. If you do decide to do that, it would be a good idea to relax together over a nice lunch before returning to the office. In fact, it would be a good idea, though not essential, to go for lunch afterwards – have a relaxing environment to reflect together and unwind – even if you do carry out the half-day on site.

❑ Of course, diary commitments may be such that you are holding the half-day in the afternoon, in which case a drink before going your separate ways could take place.

❑ You will be the best judge of location and whether it would help to have an informal continuation of the event.

❑ Finally, it may be that your team is geographically dispersed – what is termed a "virtual" team. In this case, it would make sense to have a special event, where you meet at some convenient hotel or conference centre.

– The costs of travel and accommodation will be more than offset by the value you will gain from building your virtual team into a real team and the subsequent sharp upward movement in productivity and efficiency.

– You may want to take the opportunity to have a full day. Once you have read the book, you will be able to choose how the extra time can best be spent.

– If you do this, please ensure that any socialising takes place after the event and not before. I have run quite a number of team-building/strategy events, e.g. For an entire department including junior staff and PAs, for all the executives and senior managers of a particular company, for functional departments, business areas and so on.

– Typically, they start on a Friday or a Saturday and have a half-day on the Saturday or Sunday. Invariably the half day is a waste of time, as the socialising has been too long and too liquid.

– I can recall one such event where I turned up promptly at 9 a.m. I was alone apart from the in-house administrator. People started drifting in from 9.25 onwards. The most senior executive, who was the sponsor of the event, turned up at 11 a.m. Needless to say little was done and the little that was done was not done well.

– It was scheduled to finish at 1 p.m., and actually finished at 12 p.m. It started with a bang and ended with a whimper.

– Yours should start with a bang and end with a firework display.

Author's note

You will also need your organisation to purchase sufficient additional copies of the book to enable you to give one to each team-member at the end of the workshop. There are two reasons:

1. They need to acquire the same knowledge that you have, so that they can build current or future groups of staff, for whom they become responsible, into effective teams in four hours.
2. Unless each team-member reads the next chapter, "Creating Growth from Change", the high-performance team you have created will not be sustained.

STEP 1 – CREATE THE RIGHT ENVIRONMENT

We look at:

❑   What you do.
❑   Why you do it.
❑   Case study of success.
❑   How you do it.
❑   How you ensure momentum is maintained.

WHAT YOU DO

❑   You tell the group, having confirmed the purpose of the morning/afternoon, that: "In this first exercise we are going to share from our experiences of working in an effective team (any team – work, school project, sports, social, whatever – in our past) what were all the *attitudes* we adopted and *actions* we took when we were in that team."

❏ The above does not have to all be written down. It is critically important that, throughout, you use the style and approach with which you are comfortable.

❏ You could simply write on the flip-chart, "Attitudes and "Actions" or add other key words – like "Any Team", "Sharing", "Experience".

❏ The reason is that I use "any team" is because many people may not have experienced a really bonded and effective group in the work-place, but most have outside work.

Author's notes

❏ As mentioned at the start of this chapter, I have run training or development programmes for over 5000 employees, varying from night-shift printers and PAs through all levels of seniority including CMDUs (Core Decision-Making Units) of large corporates.

❏ When I have asked them the question as to whether they go to work with a song in their heart as they are about to rejoin their high-energy high-performing team, the universal reply is, "NO"

❏ Indeed the vast majority go further and tell me that they find the endless meetings they have to attend a "pain in the backside", a complete waste of time and they are fed up having to catch up, by working late to complete all their numerous assignments.

❏ I realised, when reflecting before writing up this chapter, that the subconscious collective mindset that is universal is that "the individual creates the team" – hence no effective team-working at work.

❏ I also realised that this inappropriate mindset consisted of four separate myths, all of which I had exploded, enabling me to develop the recipe. Specifically:

1. The focus on individual personalities and differences. This causes "blood on the carpet" and denies effective team-working ever taking place.

2.   The focus on the individual's role within the team, e.g. Belbin's "plant", who is the most creative individual. This denies any learning, acerbates "personality clashes" and means that the group cannot produce any synergy – where the sum of the individual parts is less than the whole the team produces. This again denies effective team-working ever taking place.

3.   Where the team-builder is an external facilitator, the received wisdom (to justify his or her fee) is that they are ever-present. This means that the group can never become "self-managing" and an unhealthy dependence on the facilitator is created. This, yet again, denies effective team-working ever taking place. [You, of course, are an internal team-builder or co-ordinator and so will be ever-present.]

4.   Throwing the individuals in the group into the deep-end with some horrendous "team-building" exercise. This guarantees, as rivers of blood start to flow, that the individuals and the group promptly sink without trace. This, once more, denies effective team-working ever taking place.

❑   Now Piaget once wrote:"*Group work is truly individualising*". He was not quite right. The truth of the matter is that "*The high-performing team creates the individual*" – the absolute reversal of "received wisdom".

WHY YOU DO IT

❑   You are starting at the end, i.e. you are getting everyone at the start of the team-building process to commit to the behaviours individuals exhibit at the end, when operating in successful or high-performing teams.

❑   You are focussing on the critical determinant of success, i.e. how we behave towards to each other, what is often termed the "culture", in which we operate.

❑   You are basing discovery on sharing – a key feature of any effective team.

❑   You are sharing from experience, rather than giving theoretical input. Recapturing a positive experience is much more powerful

for the individual than any theoretical input.
- ❑ By starting at the end, you ensure that you will reach the end rapidly (more or less straightaway).
- ❑ The repetition and reinforcement of the right behaviours over a four-hour period means that they become embedded.

CASE STUDY OF SUCCESS

From tears to happiness

About a decade ago now, I was running a management development programme that was split into two modules, about three or four months apart.

The climax of the first module, when all the groups had become effective teams and so were willing to open up to each other, was for each team-member to share their deepest concerns and we would use the power of the team to try to resolve them.

It will come as no surprise to you that it is problems in relationships that universally cause the most stress and headaches for the individual, rather than the work itself.

Janice, we will call her, had a dual role. She was a PA in a pod system but also the manager of the pod, i.e. had 5 PAs to look after.

Penny had lost her best mate as the result of a secretarial review a few months earlier and had become demotivated and isolated from the rest of the team. Her performance was variable and she behaved irrationally a lot of the time – aggressive to passive and back again.

The whole team was affected. Janice had tried to adopt a calm considerate approach and had had quite a number of 1-on-1s with Penny which got nowhere. Either Janice was in danger of losing her own cool at the aggressive response or was faced with a woman weeping uncontrollably.

She had contemplated involving HR and starting the disciplinary process, but knew that, if she did, she would get a black mark for failing to be a competent manager. She was at her wits' end.

As a result of the group's input, Janice decided to stop "knocking her head against the Penny brick wall" and carry out the attitudes and

From tears to happiness

actions exercise that she had done at the beginning of the programme – for the whole team.

She did and reported back at the beginning of the second module. Not total success, but a giant leap forward. Penny was now part of the team, who were performing much better as a unit. Penny still had occasional mood swings but these were tolerated by the team. Penny's overall performance had gone up considerably.

From Penny's point of view, she was part of a process or exercise that included everyone – not an individual being "picked on". This is, of course, the power of a team approach.

No individual blame produces maximum team gain.

HOW YOU DO IT

- ❏ This may seem a strange question, but it isn't. As coordinator, you will be the focus of attention, as you will be the scribe and writing the answers of the group on the flip chart. You will be contributing, but your key role is to ask questions.
- ❏ You see, what happens is that groups tend to find it easier to come up with an attitude than an action. For instance, someone might say: "show each other respect". Great, that is an excellent attitude to have and is one that is the hall-mark of effective teams, i.e. mutual respect.
- ❏ It is actions that determine outcomes. So, you may need to ask the group. "Excellent – but how do we show respect?" Someone will answer: "We need to listen to each other".
- ❏ It is much easier, when someone is not listening, for someone else to say (in a warm tone of voice). "We all agreed that we would listen to each other – so could you please listen to me". "Sorry, of course I will".
- ❏ It is much tougher for the individual to take an "attack" on an attitude that they are no longer displaying, e.g. "You are not showing me respect" or, in modern parlance, "You are dissing me."

❏ Whenever I have facilitated this exercise, I have simply accepted the presentations made by the different groups, unless there is a vital action missing.

❏ In the work-books, we put together the following template:

Attitudes	Actions
Trust	Sharing
Honesty	Creating safe, confidential environment
Respect	Listening
Interest	Staying focused and contributing
Humility	Trying out other's ideas
Openness	Altering opinions
Support	Praising and encouraging
Co-operation	Suppressing ego
Challenge	Questioning
Reflection	Planning

❏ You and your group may come up with more or less. There is no need to have a perfect correlation with one attitude producing one action. It is a process that can evolve. You can add or subtract to the list as the result of experience.

❏ As long as key elements are there, that is fine. Generally speaking, groups tend to have one important omission and make one mistake.

Omission

❏ The omission tends to be "challenge". I can understand that, as "challenge" is a confrontational word – the only confrontational attitude in this particular list.

❏ If I am the facilitator, I don't mention the word "challenge". What I say is that it would a good idea if they added to the list of actions – that they should ask questions, as that is the key to learning and discovery.

Mistake

Many, many groups either put up that they should provide "constructive criticism" or the gentler "politically correct" phrase "give feedback". This is an absolute no no. This is proved in the next case study – learning from experience

Learning from experience

In 1985, I attended a two-week team-building programme run for bank staff. I decided that I would not be my normal arrogant intellectual self, but, drawing from the list on the previous page, would show respect, humility, support and co-operate. In terms of actions, "listen, try out other's ideas, praise and encourage, and suppress ego".

I was successful, in that our team was the only team of the three that made it to a cohesive, high-performing unit.

On the final Thursday afternoon, we were told by our tutors to go to our syndicate rooms and write down everything we liked and disliked about our fellow team-members, and distribute our sheets of paper around.

We decided to keep the negatives to one and accentuate all the positives and so came out psychologically unscathed.

However, there was one individual, we will call Richard, who was a member of one of the other groups, who never made the "commitment" level.

Now, during the fortnight, every team-member had had the opportunity to be the leader of one of the many projects we carried out.

Richard thought that he was a brilliant leader – but had, in fact, been useless – basically been the "big boss" – not listening to anyone, ignoring others' ideas and ordering people about. So, having been given permission by these team-destroying tutors, they all wrote this down in great detail and handed it to the poor unfortunate.

Most of us have gaps between our conscious self-image and view of ourselves (accentuating the positive) and the whole truth. We tend to have the darker side of our natures lurking in our subconscious as

Learning from experience

negative forces that drive action without conscious control or recognition of bad behaviour. If you like, many of us believe ourselves consciously to be Dr Jekylls and not recognise our hidden My Hydes.

Now, if Richard had had but a single piece of paper from one individual saying, "you are a very Hydeous", he would have rejected it outright (too much damage to conscious self-image and confidence levels) and "shot the messenger" – in fact, accused the messenger of the same faults, he could not see in himself.

Poor Richard had 6 other people simultaneously telling him that he was the opposite of what he believed himself to be. He simply could not handle it. He got very drunk indeed, damaged some furniture and then physically assaulted a member from another training programme being run at the Centre. He was subsequently "let go".

Key Point

So you need to ensure that the group accepts that there should be a "No Blame" rule (to avoid the negative) as wells as "Praising and Encouraging" to accentuate the positive

HOW YOU ENSURE MOMENTUM IS MAINTAINED

❑ The key question you ask your group is: "Well, that's great. We have agreed all the attitudes we are going to adopt and actions to take, but how do we ensure that we will actually carry them out?"

❑ At the end of the discussion, the answer will pop out, if necessary, after a gentle bit of steering from yourself: "Anyone in the group is given permission by all the other members to point out any breach of the rules by any member."

❑ This is an extraordinarily effective way of overcoming the drawbacks of and clashes between different personality types, without ever referring to them.

❑ Some people are not very good listeners. They need to genuinely commit to listening. If they demonstrably fail to listen and someone with a positive tone of voice and genuinely supportively points that out, they accept it without demur and with no negative feelings toward the other person.

❑ They have unintentionally broken something they want to do. They are annoyed with themselves and not the other person.

❑ What also happens, quite remarkably, is that, because the 4 hour process ensures continuation of all the positive behaviours, they start catching themselves out before they are caught up. "Oh! God, that's my ego speaking" or "I have stopped listening".

❑ Regarding timings, this session takes approximately half an hour. So the clock has moved from 09.00 to 09.30.

STEP 2 – PROMOTE GROUP DISCOVERY

Author's Note

Necessarily, there is some repetition from the section in chapter 4 covering "improving creativity". The key learning is how to develop understanding and successful application of the Group Discovery Technique (GDT) on a group and not individual basis.

INTRODUCTION

❑ The Group Discovery Technique (GDT) is the means by which each individual in the group discovers that the group can produce more and better ideas than any individual. This, as mentioned earlier, is called creative synergy.

❑ For it to be successful you follow a simple process, i.e. a set of rules/activities in a time sequence, and continue to follow the behaviours to which each individual is now committed.

❑ It is extraordinarily powerful, because it converts the most cynical and sceptical individual to the fact that the team is more effective than the individual.

❑ All of you will have heard of the word "brainstorming". There are two drawbacks to "brainstorming".

1. Terminology.
2. Application in real life.

1. TERMINOLOGY

Brainstorming is a right-brained word that subconsciously irritates left-brained people. Indeed, I ran a workshop recently, building a group of four comic actors into a team using the recipe, and none of them liked the word – and they are all right-brained! Incidentally, the quote this group provided on this workshop was: *"It's revolutionised the way we work and has improved us as a team 150%."*

2. APPLICATION IN REAL LIFE

- ❑ When I am promoting discovery of the first two rules of GDT, I ask the groups if they have ever been in a team-meeting, where they have been asked to contribute ideas as part of a "brainstorming session". A universal "Yes".
- ❑ I then ask what happens in real life. Invariably someone will say that their idea was ridiculed or criticised.
- ❑ I then ask what the consequence of that criticism is. The answer is that they stop contributing their ideas.
- ❑ I then ask what the outcome of this "brainstorming session" is. The reply is "the one right answer."
- ❑ I then ask who provides "the one right answer". The answer is the BOSS.

I now turn to:

- ❑ The four rules of GDT.
- ❑ Testing.
- ❑ The outcomes produced.
- ❑ Ensuring you stay true to your own style.
- ❑ Creative thinking scenarios.

THE FOUR RULES OF GDT

1. Separate out exploration from evaluation.
2. Stamp on criticism.
3. Help develop other's ideas.
4. Be creative on assumptions.

1. Separate out exploration from evaluation

❑ You will come to the evaluation stage when you are applying the process to progress your key strategic issue in the next step.

❑ When you apply and prove the power of GDT in the testing phase in this step, remember that there will be no evaluation – you will stay in exploration or creative mode.

Author's notes

❑ You will find that, in the testing phase, you will get a whole range of answers (all of them "right answers") and, in the example provided before testing, the group produced a quantum leap, as an answer.

❑ There was no formal evaluation phase because the next rule, "Stamp on Criticism", was rigorously upheld.

❑ The point is, when you are in purely creative mode, you don't know where it will lead you – the nature and the beauty of exploration only.

2. Stamp on criticism

This is critical to avoid the "one right answer". It is also critically important to stamp on non-verbal as well as verbal criticism. As body language contributes 55% to effective communication, a look to the ceiling or a shrug of the shoulders are just as effective as a critical comment with a harsh tone of voice.

3. Help develop others' ideas

❑ Synergy is not achieved by pooling individual suggestions, but by building on them through open questions, so that there is a flow of ideas and, hence, potential solutions. The individual should think of their idea as a gift to the group to be changed from silver into gold – not as something that must be jealously guarded and protected: *"Because it's my idea, not yours. My idea is bigger than yours."*

❑ I use the Alaskan Electricity example of the first three rules in action, which I now repeat.

Alaskan Electricity Company

The Alaskan Electricity Company faced terrible problems in the 1970s. It managed over 1000 miles of over ground telegraph poles, supplying electricity to a sparse and widely scattered population in very hostile weather conditions.

As a result of the terrible weather, ice and snow gathered on the overhead cables, which frequently snapped under the weight. Teams of men had to travel miles and miles to repair these cables. The costs of such operations exhausted all their profits.

The company solved the problem through a group of people questioning effectively and following the three rules. These are the questions:

- ❑ Why not shake the poles?
- ❑ How do we shake the poles?
- ❑ Why not use polar bears?
- ❑ How do we motivate the bears to shake the poles?
- ❑ Why not put meat on top of the poles?
- ❑ How do we get meat on top of the poles?
- ❑ Why not use a helicopter?
- ❑ Why not forget about the bears and use the whirring blades of the helicopter to get rid of the snow and ice, before it forms?

And that is what the Alaskan Electricity Company did – with considerable cost saving. Prevention was cheaper than cure.

Key points

- ❑ As mentioned in chapter 4, there was a logical connection between the open, exploring "how" question and the actual idea or suggestion prefaced by "why not". Logical, practical people often label themselves as not being very creative. Provided you suspend judgement and do not criticise yourself, logical people can be extremely creative.
- ❑ Indeed, if you accept my definition of intuition as the

"subconscious learning from experience that rests in the subconscious", then I would argue that learning is a processing of the experience, i.e. thinking logically with connected steps as in the above. The subconscious brain obeys the first two rules. This is why, if we sleep on a problem, the subconscious brain may solve it for us.

❑ If you practise this approach to creative problem-solving (on your own as an individual), you will become more intuitive and a quantum leaper.

❑ Clearly criticism would have killed the solution stone dead. Those who criticise always have to give a reason. So we would have had comments along the lines of:

– "Why not shake the poles?" – "What a stupid impractical idea?"
– "Why not use polar bears?" – "How ridiculous. I have done my research and there are 3 million poles and 650 polar bears."
– "Why not put meat on top of the poles?" – "How stupid can you get? The polar bears would smash the wires in the attempt to get the meat."

❑ There was a clear "helping others' ideas", which is why a very neat solution emerged so quickly. The group achieved a quantum leap, and, as mentioned before, so can you individually.

❑ The final point is that this was a specific, concrete problem and, in this case, GDT produced an excellent solution achieved by purely using open questions.

❑ When you are addressing your strategic issue in the next session, GDT will produce a whole range of ideas, which the group will need to evaluate as part of the process. Clearly there can be a neat solution to the specific "snow and ice problem" but a range of "answers" to an issue like "changing culture effectively" – the most important of which can be implemented through the appropriate projects.

4. Be creative on assumptions
[Again, there is an inevitable degree of repetition from chapter 4]
   We look at:

- ❏ The reason for the rule
- ❏ Application of the rule

Reason for the rule

- ❏ Daily life requires that we make assumptions. However, trainers often point that, if we ASSUME, we are making an "ASS" out of "U" and "ME".
- ❏ Problem-solving demands that we identify and question our unconscious assumptions. Indeed, we should be creative on assumptions – not close down by asking the question: *"What are all the assumptions we are making"* but open up by asking the group the question: *"What are all the possible assumptions we could be making?"*
- ❏ I demonstrate the power of this creative approach to assumptions by taking one of the creative thinking scenarios, used to practice GDT in the test phase. They used to be called "Lateral Thinking Questions."
- ❏ Originally, designers of these questions designed them thinking that there was only one right answer and trying to ensure that there was only one right answer.
- ❏ So the tutor would say to the groups. Here is a problem, "A man sold his dog and was killed on the way home". Now what is the answer to this problem? You will have to think "laterally" (or *"outside the box"* these days) in order to find it.
- ❏ So off the groups would go, or just work silently on their own in situ, and then one individual would shout out. *"Sir, Sir, I'm so very, very clever. I'm the bestest little creative thinker in the group. Ya! Boo! Sucks to You! – all you inferior people in my team or in this room. The answer is. "He was blind. He had sold his guide dog."*
- ❏ This did not do a power of good to the development of a high-performing team!

Application of the rule

- ❏ We now look at the creative thinking scenario: "a man sold his dog and was killed on the way home."

Build an Effective Team Very Rapidly

□ As regards to the answers, it is critically important that you use the 4th rule, "be creative on assumptions", to increase the range of answers.
□ Now to a range of assumptions and answers:

– It could have been a very valuable dog, and the man was mugged for the money and died on the way home.

– It could have been a large, angry dog, which escaped from its new owners, and carried out a fatal revenge attack on his former master.

– It could have been a particular breed of dog, e.g. a husky. The man had sold the lead dog of his sled and had fallen into a crevasse and died.

– It could have been a guide dog, as his master was blind, and the blind man had been run over on the way home – the one right answer!

– It could have been his wife's dog whom she adored much, much more than hubbie and so she had shot her husband. (This is not strictly acceptable as the creative thinking scenario refers to "his" dog – but "No criticism rules OK". In any case, it is a general rule, made by the creative guru Edward de Bono, not to define a problem too closely, if you want to avoid missing out on potentially fantastic solutions. The problem would have been better put: "A man sold a dog and was killed on the way home," in which case there are many more solutions.)

– If you study the phrasing, there is nothing to stop you interpreting the sentence as to mean that the dog was killed on the way home – run over, eaten, killed by another dog and so on.

– You can argue that there is no connection between the two and then come up with as many answers as you like as to why a man should be killed on the way home!

TESTING

Now, what I say to the groups before they go off to practice GDT is:

Remember all the GDT rules

□ If I have not promoted discovery of the rules, I always ensure the group(s) repeat them twice so that they have "sunk in". This is very important, as you want to minimise or eradicate any breaches, particularly of the no-criticism rule.

❑   This has become custom and habit to-left brained people and you don't want them to have to be told off for what is always an unintentional breach.

❑   Paradoxically, left-brained people love the word "rule" and once they have sunk in, they become great allies and drivers towards success, as they make sure all the rules are followed.

❑   They not only ensure that the no criticism rule is followed by all, but stop the right-brained people getting out of kilter – dashing ahead and coming up with their ideas on a creative thinking scenario that is not yet being considered by the group as a whole.

❑   I have printed up a number of scenarios that equals the total number in the largest group and suggested that they look at them altogether sequentially. As mentioned, over-enthusiastic individuals can get ahead of themselves and diminish the effectiveness of GDT.

Appoint rotating co-ordinators

❑   This is so that everyone gets a bite at the cherry and starts the process of enabling each team-member to develop coordinating skills, which, as you know, are critical to building an effective team.

❑   I suggest, when they get into their syndicate rooms, they agree the order of co-ordinators and, once that has been established, everyone reads the question, has a few moments to absorb the information, and then the co-ordinator manages the process and writes out all the ideas on the flipchart.

Have fun

❑   Humour is the engine of creativity

Come up with as many possible ideas as you can in the time available to explain each of the scenarios you are given.

❑ I allow 5 minutes per scenario and add on an extra 5, as people get totally absorbed in the exercise and time flies out of the window.

THE OUTCOMES PRODUCED

❑ When they have come back into plenary, if there is more than one group, then the set of answers for each question are provided on the basis of the particular co-ordinator leading the answers to the particular scenario with the other group's coordinators only adding additional solutions.

❑ I then rotate the lead co-ordinator so that total fairness is seen to prevail. There is an almost universal desire to be treated fairly, whatever the age or seniority of the individual.

Author's note
My own view is that, unintentionally, a parent or parents preached fairness and practiced unfairness when the adults were children.

❑ I must say that managing the feedback process is by far the most complicated matter for me, as I am having to multi-task, which is not a natural strength. I am delighted when I am dealing with only one group.

❑ I then ask three questions:

1. **Does any individual in the room think that there would have been more ideas produced if you had gone away on your own to solve the problems?**
   The answer is a universal "no". So I point out that they have just experienced group creative synergy, i.e. The number of the ideas the group comes up with exceeds the sum of all the ideas, each individual would have come up, thinking on their own.

2. **Was it just the one individual who came up with all the answers, or was it shared?**
   The universal answer is "shared".

3. So what does that prove?

Total silence usually follows this question. Whenever "promoting discovery" – my preferred approach – fails, I am more than happy to provide the "one right answer". My answer is: "It proves the point I made earlier that every individual can become more creative thanks to the power of GDT."

Author's notes

❑ As mentioned before, I have used the full recipe or the vital first two steps with over 1,000 groups with staff varying from PAs and night-shift printers through managers, senior managers, and executives to CDMUs (Core Decision-Making Units).

❑ These groups have been located in UK, US, Hong Kong, Thailand and Malaysia. With all the cultural diversity that exists in most countries, there has been a very wide range of "countries of origin" within a given country location for the programme.

❑ One client was located in 27 different countries. As the programmes were "global", we had an extraordinary range of different cultures represented.

❑ What was particularly enjoyable was "converting" one group of highly intellectual, left-brained, cynical and sceptical lawyers.

❑ There has been a 99.9% success rate in terms of achieving synergy and everyone agreeing to that outcome, with all the beneficial psychological impact that has, i.e. creating a belief in real team-working.

ENSURE YOU STAY TRUE TO YOUR OWN STYLE

❑ This is a continuing theme. I am not asking you to: "act out of character".

❑ You may be a "tell merchant", in which case tell them the rules, but remember to ensure the two-times repetition (three times mentioned in all) so that the messages have "sunk in".

❑ You may be a "promoting discovery" merchant. In which case, "promote discovery".

❑ You may be somewhere in between, in which case cover GDT with a mixture.

❑ I can assure you that it works, whichever approach you adopt, though the "promoting discovery" approach takes longer.

❑ I favour the "promoting discovery" approach. However, on many development programmes for my clients, I have worked with one of my team of trainers that I recruited as my business expanded. I prefer to go solo, but many clients like to have diversity for their participants.

❑ I had one such trainer in my team, who was flexible by nature. This meant that he left everything to the last minute and did not show the same respect to time-tables, as a born organiser like my good self did.

❑ The GDT session, which I always ran, was the last session before lunch. In addition to the "attitude and actions" session, there was a house-keeping session, as well as time taken out to identify individual needs.

❑ So I lost a good half an hour on occasions, and simply did a rather rapid "tell" session with no adverse effect on outcomes.

❑ My suggestion would be that you put the four rules on a prepared flip-chart, the questions in the Alaskan Electricity Example, and have a typed up hand-out of the creative thinking scenarios.

❑ You can cover the man and his dog scenario on the hoof or, if you have an artistic bent, draw a picture of a stick man and dog or even a little cartoon. First man with dog, then man without dog, then dead man.

❑ I used to do this very occasionally on the hoof (when I had the time) rather than pre-prepared. It acted as a sudden and pleasant diversion from what had gone before and, as I cannot draw for toffee and my dog more often than not looked like a sheep, it generated some humour at my expense (I took it like a man). It was a good thing to do, as humour is the engine of creativity, and so it helped generate the right mood and ambience.

Author's notes

❑ I used the man and his dog as the example of "being creative on assumptions" when applying the recipe to a group of four – three comic actors and their creative writer.

❑ I got rid of the "his" in front of the dog and it worked a treat. My drawing of the dog still has not improved with the passage of time! I used the comic strip approach.

❑ As to timings, I would set aside an hour and a quarter. Taking into account the half an hour for the "attitude and actions" session, the end of the GGT session marks the quarter of an hour coffee break.

❑ I conclude this section with 21 more creative thinking scenarios and would mention that all age ranges from children aged 4 upwards absolutely love them.

Key point
You only hand out the same number of scenarios as there are group members. The rest you keep up your sleeve.

CREATIVE THINKING SCENARIOS

1. A little girl, standing with her 2 parents by a river, looks at their reflection in the water, and says: "I can see all four of us". There are only three people present.

2. A woman, in despair, throws herself from the top of a skyscraper. It is a deliberate act of suicide. As she tumbles down, she hears a telephone ring, and cries out: "I wish I had not jumped".

3. A woman enters a field, and immediately dies. The pack on her back is empty.

4. A man stood looking through the window on the sixth floor of an office building. Suddenly, he was overcome by an impulse. He opened the window and leapt through it. He did not use a parachute or land on water or any special soft surface. Yet the man was completely unhurt when he landed.

5. Five men were proceeding down a country path. It began to rain. Four of the men quickened their step and began to walk faster. The fifth man made no effort to move any faster. However, he remained dry and the other four got wet. They all arrived at their destination together.

6. A policeman was called because a man was found lying

unconscious outside a shop. As soon as the man came around, he was arrested. He was not a known criminal and had not been engaged in any kind of fight or dispute before losing consciousness.

7. A man and his golden retriever dog were found dead in the middle of a field. The man was wearing wading boots. No one else was around.

8. On a busy Friday afternoon, a man walked several miles across London from Westminster to Knightsbridge without being seen by anybody. The day was clear and bright. He did not travel by any method of transport other than by foot. London was thronged with people, yet not one of them saw him.

9. A man in a restaurant complained to the waiter that there was a fly in his cup of coffee. The waiter took the cup away and promised to bring a fresh cup of coffee. He returned a few moments later. The man tasted the coffee and complained that this was his original cup of coffee with the fly removed. He was correct.

10. A deserted yacht is found floating in the middle of the ocean and around it in the water are a dozen human corpses. There is no danger aboard the yacht and the yacht is not defective.

11. A farmer has two pigs. He sells them both on the same day at the same market, and each was sold for a fair price. Yet, when he sells them he gets 100 times more for one than the other.

12. A woman knocked on a stranger's door and asked to use the bathroom. She came out and killed the man with an axe.

13. A swimmer swam the 100 metre freestyle in a new world record. The pool, water and ambient conditions were all acceptable. The record was not allowed to stand.

14. Two frogs fell into a large cylindrical tank of cream and both fell to the bottom. The walls were sheer and slippery. One frog died but one survived.

15. A young girl was listening to the radio. Suddenly it went off for a minute, and then came back on again. There was nothing wrong with the radio or with the programme transmission from the radio station. She did not touch the radio controls.

16. A man is lying dead in a telephone booth. The telephone is off the hook, dangling down. Two of the windows are broken. He was not murdered.

17. A woman lies awake unable to sleep. She makes a telephone call. 5 minutes later she is asleep.
18. A man watched his wife plunge head first down a deep ravine. He returned home to find her taking their dinner out of the microwave, completely unhurt.
19. A man is pushing a car, which stops next to a hotel. The man realises he is bankrupt.
20. An archaeological team discover two, very well-preserved corpses, whilst excavating. The next day the newspapers proclaim: "Positive identification of Adam and Eve".
21. A naked man is found dead in a desert, clutching a straw. There are hills not far away and nothing but sand in the immediate vicinity.

STEP 3: HARNESS THE POWER OF PROCESS

❑ This is the really meaty exercise, which takes up about half the time. It is where you use a very carefully designed process to progress your most important strategic issue into an action plan or plans which your team members will be enthusiastically committed to implement.
❑ What we will do is:

   – Set out the complete process.
   – Provide a real-life example of success.
   – Analyse each step of the process.
   – Consider the process to determine process
   – We then look at the final short session – the review.

SET OUT THE COMPLETE PROCESS

1. **Identify a single strategic issue that you/your group is interested in developing**
   e.g. We will improve our work/life balance.
2. **Develop statement of intent with time-frame**
   e.g. In two years, we will have achieved an effective work/life balance.

3. **Determine what success looks like**
   What will it look/feel like operating with an effective work/life balance? What will be happening that will guarantee that we have an effective work/life balance?
4. **Determine how to measure success**
   What quantifiable measure or measures should be introduced so that we know that we have achieved an effective work/life balance?
5. **Determine what needs to be done to achieve success**
   Use GDT to come up with as many ideas/suggestions as possible that will create an effective work/life balance.
6. **Agree the top 4 priorities for implementation**
   – Each individual in the group determines the 4 priorities they would personally select for implementation, allocating 4 points to their first choice, 3 to their second, 2 to their third and 1 to their last choice.
   – When every individual has made their decision, each comes to the flip-chart and puts the number against the ideas selected.
   – The top 4 ideas have the highest aggregate totals.
7. **Develop the process plan in each priority area**
   For each priority area, determine:
   – What should be done first and why?
   – What should be done second and why? and so on.
   – Then complete each plan by putting approximate timings for the sequence of activities.

Author's notes

❑   I have taken this from the brief on the process in a work-book. Of course, you would not need an hour and three quarters to solve this particular issue. Roughly 10 seconds.

❑   The answer is: "ensure that every employee in our organisation is working in an effective team in 6 months by implementing Project Omega – see final chapter, "Maximise Your Company's Profitability.""

PROVIDE AN EXAMPLE OF SUCCESS

❑ A number of my clients asked me to apply this process model with groups of their managers on a given programme. The managers would be provided with the key strategic issues the company had identified as part of their overall game plan.

❑ They would then select an issue and progress it through to an action plan, which would be typed up and sent to the CEO – a very neat way of getting effective input into strategy development.

❑ I have had a number of City Law firms in the past as clients and this is the presentation made by one of the groups of associate lawyers who completed the process. The programme was run in 2002.

Example

1. Identify a single strategic issue that your group is interested in developing.

❑ Retaining high quality associates.

2. Develop statement of intent with time-frame.

❑ By May 2004, new system in place.
❑ By May 2006, results outlined (in point 3) below obtained.

3. Determine what success looks like.

❑ Deliver higher quality of work to clients.
❑ Increase in profitability.
❑ Higher morale among associates at all levels.
❑ Retain more high quality senior associates.

4. Determine how to measure success.

❑ Improved retention rate among identified high value associates.

Example

- Has profitability increased?
- Has morale improved (associate/partner survey)?
- Have we delivered high quality work?
- Client buy in.

5. How to achieve success:

- Establish distinct career path for senior associates that is an alternative to (but neither a bar nor a necessary precursor to) partnership.
- Implement genuinely flexible remuneration and reward package for senior associates (currently there appears to be little or no flexibility in practice).
- Have transparent policy on senior associate career path.

6. Process plan:
a. Distinct career path

- Consultation among partners, associates and clients.
- Research into how our and other firms have made use of counsel positions – lessons learned.
- Determine nature of role and policy to implement.
- Pilot/test in different offices.
- Global implementation May 2006.

b. Flexible remuneration

- Research packages at other law firms (inc. US) and other employers.
- Seek feedback from senior associates.
- Determine what can be flexible, in terms of pay and other benefits.
- Committee of partners, HR and senior associates draft transparent policy.

> ## Example
>
> ❑ Finalise policy.
> ❑ Follow policy in practice through consultation with senior associates.
>
> c. Policy on career path
> ❑ Consultation with senior associates.
> ❑ Committee of partners, HR and senior associates draft policy.
> ❑ Finalise policy and publish on intranet.
> ❑ Annual meetings (separate from appraisals) among each senior associate, a partner (not necessarily line manager) and an HR representative to assess progress by reference to the policy.

Author's notes

❑ You will note that step 7 has become step 6 as the voting for priorities has not been recorded. Rightly, senior executives are not interested in how their managers decided on the priorities, only on the results. So we never typed this up.
❑ However, I provide an example of the voting system in action for a decision-making unit in the next section.

ANALYSE EACH STEP OF THE PROCESS
1. Identify a single strategic issue that you/your group is interested in developing

Two questions arise:

❑ Why a single issue?
❑ How to decide which issue?

Why a single issue?

❑ I have noticed that, if two people focus in their discussion on a single issue, they, typically, get their act together, progress the problem and finish the conversation on a high with a commitment to meet up again. If there are multiple issues, then one or the other gets distracted and the conversation and the relationship loses its way.

❑ The other reason to use a single issue is thanks to Sir Brian Pitman, who was appointed CEO of the then Lloyds Bank in 1983. It was the worst performing bank amongst the then big four clearers – Lloyds, Barclays, Midland and NatWest. In the period 1983 – 1989, he increased profits by an annual average of 30% and Lloyds Bank became the best-performing (i.e. most profitable) clearer. His quote to me, as mentioned in the second chapter, was: *"Effective strategy requires focus and hard choices."*

❑ The need for a single issue is not generally recognised. This is the issue that the particular group selected to consider:
"Recruiting, training, developing and retaining the brightest and best-motivated graduates to maintain the quality of the firm"

❑ When I pointed out the importance of focusing on a single issue, they chose the one, naturally, in which they had most personal interest.

How to decide which issue?

❑ I would imagine that this will spring out, as everyone will know and it will be your most important issue. What many leaders fail to realise is that not only do "great minds think alike" but so too do a collection of great minds, i.e. team minds think alike.

❑ Brian Edwards, the Managing Director of St. Ives plc, when he had experienced the St Ives development programme, came up with the excellent quote: *"An effective leader or coach provides motivation on a voyage of discovery, where common sense prevails"*. Effective group working enables the discovery of that common sense.

❑ Two case studies illustrate this key point:

Ask the right question

A large insurance company recognised that, to survive and grow in rapidly changing market conditions, it would have to change its customer base and distribution channels – two very significant changes.

So the Board spent 6 months developing its strategy in considerable detail. They were poised to roll out the strategy, when a junior board member asked the right question. "We know that we have developed the best strategy, but how are we going to motivate our senior managers to implement it?"

Their response was remarkable and remarkably effective. They flew all their senior managers to Copenhagen for 3 days, split them up into teams, and presented them with the problems and all the research findings – but none of the Board's strategy.

There were two outcomes:

1. They came up with the same strategic response.
2. They were fully motivated to implement it, which they did. This included some of those managers making themselves redundant!

Leading from behind

I and a colleague ran a three-day strategy development and team-building programme for the then DERA (Defence and Research Agency). The programme was run for Sir John Chisholm, the CEO, and the top 32 decision-takers in the various businesses.

What was very interesting about this programme was that Sir John had developed a very clear view beforehand of the vision, strategic direction and key actions required. At the end of the programme, all the teams had developed exactly the same view – but they had discovered it for themselves and so were committed to it.

It is an example of effective leadership, as defined by Dwight Eisenhower: "Leadership is the art of getting someone else to do something you want done because they want to do it". Sir John Chisholm is now Chairman of the Medical Research Council.

However, if there is a lack of clarity amongst the group, then you can use the process set out under step 6, to which we will come shortly.

2. Develop statement of intent with time-frame

❑ The phrase "statement of intent" has been used deliberately. Typically, Western companies use left-brained words like goals, objectives and targets, which result in hard measures and too narrow a focus, all of which does nothing to motivate the employee.

❑ You may be aware that the Japanese grew from small local players to global giants. The first thing they did was to form a "statement of strategic intent", e.g. Komatsu's "statement of strategic intent" was to "encircle Caterpillar", and it was successful.

❑ These could be 20 years out, but were used to focus all the employees on a single motivational goal ("beat the competition").

❑ They then set a series of "Corporate Challenges" – what we in the West refer to as interim milestones. Employees are much more motivated to "rise to a challenge" than aim for a milestone.

❑ A corporate challenge was set, typically, for a three-year period, one all the employees could easily relate too – not too far away on the horizon. The first corporate challenge selected was the one that would be most effective in achieving the "strategic intent". It was, for all the Japanese companies, to provide total quality.

❑ Now, interestingly, the Japanese operated a system called Keretsu. This was nationwide and meant that all companies in a given industry (and across industries) shared knowledge and the development of the appropriate technology to make the given dream come true.

❑ With our excessively competitive industries, very little of that was going on (no critical mass of investment developing) and, of course, there was no united front or focus within a given company.

❑ Hence the successful "zero defects" policy and the "just-in-time" delivery systems and the eradication of our indigenous motor car manufacturing industry to name but one.

3. Determine what success looks like
This is whole-brained, combining a mission and a vision. If you look

back to the lawyers' answers we have:

Mission

❑   Increase in profitability

Vision

❑   Deliver higher quality of work to clients
❑   Higher morale among associates at all levels
❑   Retain more high quality senior associates

Author's note
Left-brained lawyers use "dry", "matter of fact" language to describe a right-brained vision. If they had all been Martin Luther Kings, then it would have been along the lines of: "*We have a dream, where only people who are motivated, enthusiastic and caring work for us, where our clients love us, because we love them and delight them all the time.*" ("*And where we make a small fortune as a result*" – to integrate the vision with the mission.)

4. Determine how to measure success
This combines quantitative measures for the left-brained "mission" and qualitative measures for the right-brained "vision".

5. Determine what needs to be done to achieve success

❑   You will find that, as you have applied GDT in the recent past, the creative momentum will be carried forward, providing, of course, the behavioural and process rules are being religiously followed.
❑   You will come up with quite a few ideas quickly and it may only take a few minutes. There is no need to prolong it, after you have run out of steam.
❑   I will take another real-life example from an intact team with 7 team-members and 3 status divisions. The strategic issue selected was, "beating the competition". I cannot recall what industry they were in, but just set out the ideas below.

1. Take them over
2. Better information
3. Improve skills
4. Better service to customers
5. Be cheaper
6. Innovate
7. Noble them
8. Cheat
9. Better advertising budget
10. One stop shop
11. Better added value
12. Use of technology
13. Let them take us over

6. Agree the top 4 priorities for implementation

❑ Each individual in the group determines the 4 priorities they would personally select for implementation, allocating 4 points to their first choice, 3 to their second, 2 to their third and 1 to their last choice.

❑ When every individual has made their decision, each comes to the flip-chart and puts the number against the ideas selected.

❑ The top 4 ideas have the highest aggregate totals.

Key points

❑ This process was the only thing of value that I gained from a day and a half's attendance at some workshop on some "unique" approach to creative thinking, given by an individual whose name I cannot recall. It was during 1996 to 1997. I have quite a good memory, but it is, as all are, selective.

❑ Its value is that it accords with the principles of effective team-working, i.e. sharing decision-taking rather than the traditional approach of the leader making the decisions.

The example

❑ The seven-man team applied step six to produce the following, with the individual rankings and total scores at the end of each idea.

1. Take them over
2. Better information (see note at end)
3. Improve skills (2,2,2,1,1,3 = 9)
4. Better service to customers (4,4,4,3,2,3 = 20)
5. Be cheaper
6. Innovate (3,3,2,4,4,2 = 18)
7. Noble them
8. Cheat
9. Better advertising budget (1)
10. One stop shop (3)
11. Better added value (2,4,4 = 10)
12. Use of technology (1,1,3,2,1 = 8)
13. Let them take us over

Note

❑   During the marking process, one team-member pointed out that they could use technology to get information on competitors and all agreed the information marks could be subsumed into the technology idea.
❑   We now summarise the top ideas, with total marks allocated in brackets.
❑   Better service to customers (20)
❑   Innovate (18)
❑   Better added value (10)
❑   Improve skills (9)
❑   Use of technology (8)
❑   It is interesting to note that the top five ideas represented 93% of the marks allocated – confirming the point about achieving consensus.
❑   This particular group, having studied the results, decided that the team as a whole would focus on driving through better service to customers (the starting point being asking customers to determine current performance in all the service elements, and which were

most important to them) with individuals/sub-groups, who had the sub-issue as a personal choice, focusing on developing them.

❏ At that time, I had not developed the full 7-step process model (it was only 4) and so they did not carry out the final step 7.

7. Develop the process plan in each priority area

For each priority area, determine:

❏ What should be done first and why?

❏ What should be done second and why? and so on.

❏ Then complete each plan by putting approximate timings for the sequence of activities.

TIMINGS

❏ One and three quarter hours is given for this session. As with the GDT session, groups get totally absorbed in this exercise – especially as it is dealing with the real thing – resolving an important strategic issue, which, if done well , which it will be, means you have all taken a giant step forward in terms of increasing both efficiency and effectiveness of output.

❏ It may be that you can complete action plans (a process plan is simply determining the right actions in the right time order) for all the top four or five priority areas. Maybe only one.

❏ The minimum goal is to achieve a process plan for the number one priority, before calling a halt at 12.45. I have never come across a group that has not achieved that – but either take on yourself or allocate the role to a group member of "watching the clock", having agreed approximate timings for each of the seven steps.

❏ If you actually complete process plans in all the priority areas, then call a halt, start the review and you can have an early lunch.

CONSIDER THE PROCESS TO DETERMINE PROCESS

❏ This is not part of the exercise but is useful information. Depending on the objective, the process to achieve the objective will vary.

❏ "Necessity is the mother of invention." I was appointed the co-ordinator of the second step of a process designed to test the competence of the final group of candidates for a job as a consultant in a small but very high powered HR consultancy firm.

❏ The major exercise was a simulation, whereby the HR director, playing a client, was firstly interviewed by one candidate to identify her needs and then the group got together to see how we could meet her needs, lead by another candidate, before a different candidate went back to have another discussion with the client and so on. I was given the leadership role in the "meeting needs" part of the exercise.

❏ I had to time to prepare, whilst the first interview took place. My mind was blank for some considerable time. I knew that I had to apply some process to this task, was not quite sure what "process" meant and had not the foggiest idea as to how you found the process.

❏ The blinding flash of inspiration came. When it was my time to take up the leadership reins, I confidently strode up to the flip chart and said/wrote: "We need to agree the process we must apply to meet the client's needs". To do this, we need to decide:

– What should be done first and why?
– What should be done second and why? and so on.
– Then complete the process plan by putting approximate timings for the sequence of activities.

❏ This, of course, is step 7, in the previous section.

❏ We used this methodology to develop a ten-step process plan to complete a team task. So delighted was Brian Edwards with the success of this process that he had laminated pocket cards made up with this process on one side and the "giving praise" and "constructive criticism" processes on the other side. He distributed these to all his managers.

❏ We finish this section with this ten-step process.

1. APPOINT A CO-ORDINATOR

❏ As you are the M&L, you would appoint yourself on the first occasion. However, as has already occurred in the "Creative Thinking Scenarios" the rest of your team have had a very brief experience of co-ordination.

❑ Once the group has developed maturity, you would rotate the position to ensure that, over time, everyone has the opportunity to coordinate (or be the process facilitator).

❑ "A volunteer is worth more than 10 pressed men". The team-member who is most confident will volunteer first. By the time the individuals, who are the least confident get "Buggins' turn", they will have had many examples of success and will know how to succeed themselves.

❑ The co-ordination role is, in fact, extremely easy to carry out, once the co-ordinator realises his or her role is to facilitate process, rather than to control people. By the time another team-member takes up the co-ordination reins, all the processes will be in place to guarantee success.

2. CLARIFY THE BRIEF

This is the time to uncover those implicit, invalid assumptions. With projects, as we now know, it is usually insufficient challenge and exploration at the start that leads to confusion and poor execution. Often, in this phase, you can produce a smarter objective or find a neater way to complete the project.

3. ENSURE EVERYONE UNDERSTANDS THE BRIEF

❑ It is vital that everyone "sings from the same hymn sheet", i.e. is clear about and fully understands the brief/objective/task as refined. Remember to ask the open question, e.g. "Sheila, do you mind recapping to make sure we are all clear" (which is long form for the abrupt open question: "What is the brief?") or recap yourself and avoid the closed question: "Do we all understand the brief".

❑ Indeed before moving to the next step, it is worth asking your group as a final check; "Any final questions before we move on as it is critically important that we have the same understanding of the brief" – then pause.

4. CHECK YOUR RESOURCES

❑ Develop a provisional time plan for the rest of the planning phases, as well as implementation.
❑ Identify which individual has what skills to complete the project to a high standard.
❑ Identify any additional resource requirements over and above what is currently available.

5. INITIATE THE GROUP DISCOVERY TECHNIQUE (GDT)

❑ As the M&L, ensure the four rules are rigorously followed.

6. SELECT AT LEAST TWO IDEAS
The favourite is selected to enable the development of plan A and the reserve to enable the development of plan B, if plan A doesn't work out in practice.

7. DEVELOP AND PLAN YOUR FIRST CHOICE
Who does what, why, where and when? This is the time to allocate roles. A new role is the task manager – the individual who is best suited to manage the implementation of the plan. It could be the coordinator, who has been looking out for the team – managing the process to date – or a different individual. Whoever it is, there still needs to be a coordinator, taking the "bird's eye" view. This ensures that:

❑ The group dynamics are not damaged by the task manager focusing on the task and not the people.
❑ There is not too much divergence from the plan in the next phase.

8. TEST IT OUT
See if plan A works out in practice. If it does, excellent. If it does not, then you fall back on plan B. Depending on resource requirements for the original idea, time can be saved if both ideas are being developed, planned and tested in parallel by sub-groups.

9. REVIEW

You do this to ensure that everyone in the group fully understands who is doing what, when and why.

10. IMPLEMENT
Key Points

❑ Invariably, any group that follows this process will complete the project ahead of schedule to an extremely high standard. This is why Brian Edwards ensured the laminated cards were produced and distributed.

❑ Once the project has been completed, there should be a group review. This should be lead by the coordinator, who acts as the coach.

❑ Please do not confuse the final step review of your team-building workshop, we are about to cover, with the review on project completion. The project review is set out in Chapter 10, "Manage Effective Feedback".

STEP 4 : THE REVIEW

❑ Returning to the recipe, at 12.45, you move into the final short step – the review of the experience.

❑ To ensure you finish on a high, you only accentuate the positive. Specifically, you ask the team two questions:

1. What are all the things we have done well as a team to produce this excellent performance?
2. What should we do to perform even better as a team?

❑ This way, you ensure you: "start with a bang and finish with a firework display."

RECIPE FOR ACTION

Exercise	Outcomes	On flip-chart	Hand-outs	Time
"Attitude & Actions"	* Discovery and commitment to the behaviours of a high-performing team. * Agreement that all team-members ensure they are followed. .	Key words, e.g. *Attitudes & Actions *Any high-performing team *Sharing from experience	None	09.00 to 09.30
GDT	*Consensus on the achievement of creative group synergy. *Consensus that the individual becomes more creative by participating in GDT.	*The four rules *The Alaskan Electricity Company Questions *A dog and a man?	Creative Thinking Scenarios [same number as there are group members]	09.30 to 10.45
Break	N/A	N/A	N/A	10.45 to 11.00
Strategic Planning Process	Commitment to implement the strategic	None	The 7-step template and example of	11.00 to 12.45

Exercise	Outcomes	On flip-chart	Hand-outs	Time
	action plan or plans produced		successful use	
Team Review	Commitment by all to actions to ensure the team goes from "strength to strength"	Key questions 1. What are all the things we have done well as a team to produce this excellent performance? 2. What should we do to perform even better as a team?	None	12.45 to 13.00

Chapter 9
Create Growth from Change

INTRODUCTION
In this chapter we consider:

❑　How the individual reacts to sudden change and how to get to an even keel and eventually achieve "growth from change".

❑　How a team reacts to sudden change and how you, as the RTB (Rapid Team Builder), can ensure damage limitation and restoration to high performance.

❑　What are all the other changes that can occur and how the RTB (Rapid Team Builder)/team can effectively respond. Specifically:

　　– Varying membership at meetings.
　　– Permanent departure of team-member.
　　– Change in team-member.
　　– Change in team-leader.
　　– Resting on your laurels.

REACTING TO SUDDEN CHANGE
We start by considering what is called the reaction or transition curve, set out on the next page:

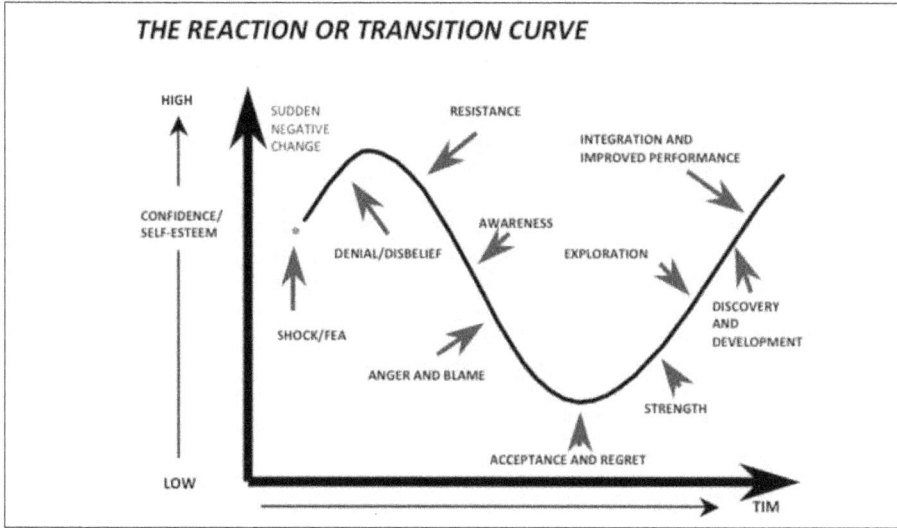

THE REACTION OR TRANSITION CURVE

REACTION OR TRANSITION CURVE

❑ I will explain the curve in some detail. We are looking at how we react to sudden negative change, the phases of reaction we go through over time, and considering the impact those phases have on our development level – combining how confident we are and how high are our feelings of self-esteem.

❑ The assumption is that we are fairly high to start with – we have quite a strong belief in our self-worth, our competence and our capability. If you like, we are quite mature.

❑ We look in time sequence at the key reactions, i.e.

 – Shock and denial
 – Resistance and awareness
 – Anger and blame
 – Acceptance
 – Exploration, discovery, and integration

SHOCK AND DENIAL

❑ The first reaction is one of shock. The suddenness, coupled with the lack of continuity, means that there is no connection with our existing mental model of reality. We have had neither prior warning nor expectation of the event. Our reaction is purely instinctive and "animal". We are caught like a rabbit in the sudden glare of the headlights of a car and freeze.

❏ We do not believe what we necessarily cannot believe – we deny the actuality that, at that moment in time, has no meaning. This is usually a short-lived phase, but not necessarily so. The key factors at play are:

– The nature of the sudden change – how severe it is.
– The degree of evidence, supporting the change.
– Our maturity.

❏ You may have noticed how the curve moves upward slightly in this phase. The reason is explained by a case study – denial.

Denial

During the 1970s recession, a large manufacturing company decided to close its least profitable plant. The plant manager called all the workers in and advised them that the plant would be closed in six months and they would all lose their jobs.

For the first three months, there was total denial, as the workers redoubled their efforts to increase productivity and stop the closure.

❏ When we are very immature, i.e. young children and, if the change is very traumatic for us, then the denial lodges permanently in our conscious selves. The unpleasant truth rests in our subconscious as an "inner demon" or "beast within". The hidden truth becomes a memory that has to be "recovered" through effective coaching so that, at last, we can be healed and complete the long-delayed journey to the "sunny uplands".

RESISTANCE AND AWARENESS

❏ Assuming that we move beyond denial, then we will resist the dawning of the new, unpleasant reality. We are starting a process of integrating the new with the old, and, initially, we have to resist so that we can close the gap slowly. It is important, when we are responsible for the shock, that we understand this and have all the evidence at our disposal to overcome this inevitable resistance.

❏ Sometimes we can be too emotional ourselves. *"Don't you believe me? I wouldn't lie to you. Are you calling me a liar!"* and so on.

❏ Resistance is also inevitable, because we are subconsciously fighting the descent to a lower level of self-esteem. When we are sacked, we lose self-esteem, we lose confidence, and our competence declines. We become more insecure. Few seek out that reality.

ANGER AND BLAME

❏ As our awareness that this change represents a new reality grows, as our resistance is overcome, we stay gripped by emotion. The emotion associated with shock is fear, an inevitable consequence of the high level of uncertainty instantly generated. Now, the emotion is one of anger and blame. We *"kick against the pricks"*, *"rail against fate"*.

❏ The anger can be both internally and externally focussed. A confident extrovert tends to blame others, and get the balance wrong. A less confident introvert tends to blame himself or herself, and gets the balance wrong.

❏ Part of self-blame that can linger into and beyond acceptance is regret. *"If only I had"*. How often do children blame themselves, their perceived incompetence and inadequacy for their parents' divorce? How often does regret for the passing of good times stay with us forever?

❏ Blame is a necessary, but fundamentally counter-productive phase, associated with the emotional response. If we are operating at a high level of self-esteem, then the blame phase tends to be temporary and not too intense.

❑ The higher our initial self-esteem, the quicker the transition and the shallower the dip in terms of loss of confidence and self-esteem. There is, unfortunately, an element of the virtuous and the vicious in our reactions to sudden negative change. The lower our self-esteem, the more vicious the reaction and the higher the more virtuous.

ACCEPTANCE

❑ Most of us will move eventually – it can be hours, days, weeks, months or years – to acceptance. However the nature of that acceptance and the extent to which it is a temporary phase on a downward or upward path will vary.

❑ Recognition of the likely reaction curve is critically important, as it enables us to move from unconscious incompetence (at the mercy of the winds of reaction, we do not recognise) to conscious competence (knowing why what is happening is happening), which significantly increases the probability that our cerebral side will intervene positively.

EXPLORATION, DISCOVERY AND INTEGRATION

❑ Provided the nature of our acceptance has a rational and positive dimension, then we will move into exploration. We have to fight to be rational; to accentuate the positive we do not feel; to seek support; to retain balance; to force out blame and replace it with detached understanding, and thereby preserve as much self-esteem as we can. We must let the heart weep (mourning is vital) but force the head to change the heart.

❑ We are complex creatures. Often we are driven by emotions, and use irrational logic to justify them. We tend to feel before we think. However, if we are prepared to listen, to explore – to open up and out – then the emotion, the intuition, will change. Intuition, after all, is the subconscious learning from experience that remains in our subconscious. If we are prepared to expose ourselves to new thoughts, new feelings, new experiences, our learning and our intuition will change.

❑ So the key to the ascent up the growth phase is to explore and evaluate from the base of acceptance – not on our own, but with others; to discover new meaning and develop new skills; to use those hidden strengths, which adversity brings closer to the surface, but which we need to consciously uncover and tap into.

❑ Finally, we need to integrate the new learning with the past, which was so suddenly changed. We need to review and reflect – to look back, not in anger, but with understanding.

HOW TEAMS REACT TO SUDDEN CHANGE

We look at exogenous shocks – sudden changes that occur from outside the team and endogenous shocks – sudden changes that occur within the team.

EXOGENOUS SHOCKS

We start with a case study – rapid transition

Rapid transistion

A group of executives on our Senior Executive Development programme were in competition with another two groups in a two-day business simulation.

This particular group had sailed through the early phases. They were carrying out the role of a subsidiary board running a pharmaceutical manufacturing company. The information had been digested and shared, the overall vision developed, a strategic plan devised, objectives set, and performance indicators and policies were in place.

They had to make quarterly decisions, spanning three years, and had input into the computer the first two sets of decisions. Delighted with the results, which exceeded expectations, the five were grouped together around the computer, having just input the third quarter decisions. They displayed all the hallmarks of a high performing team – energy, commitment, focus, humour and a very positive body language.

The results flashed up on the screen. Five pairs of eyes followed the screen down to the profit or loss for the quarter, not necessarily the

Rapid transistion

sole yardstick for success, but one that all groups treat as king. They were expecting a modest profit. They saw a thumping great loss, in excess of £250,000.

Within less than a minute, the team had totally fragmented – back to "blood on the carpet" in the twinkling of an eye.

The managing director of the group told me in no uncertain terms what he thought of the simulation. He was an extrovert, quickly accepted the evidence of "failure" and was allocating blame externally to the group.

The personnel director disappeared to the toilet. He was an introvert. The finance director went to a corner of the room, shaking his head in disbelief, clutching the print-outs to his bosom. He was also an introvert.

The production director and sales director (both extroverts) entered into a "healthy dialogue", where each blamed the other for the debacle.

Note:
What had not been taken on board by this group (with a strong task focus) was, as had been advised to them, that this was a very sophisticated simulation, which took into account all the key soft factors, as well as the hard factors.

They were brilliant at the hard staff but had neglected an important "soft factor". They had completely ignored to put into play any of the key motivational strategies for the work-force – particularly regular training and development to ensure the work-force had the right set of skills and competencies for the job.

Now, there was, both to reflect reality and to give an opportunity to catch the problem before it was too late, a delayed reaction built into the simulation. You were allowed to sin twice before the error of your ways caught up with you.

Having made the best "hard" decisions as their MD (or the guy who played the role) had produced an effective team very rapidly as already evidenced, their results were spectacular after the first two inputs. Hence the utter shock and disbelief exhibited by the MD after

Rapid transistion

the catastrophe of the £250,000 third quarter loss.

What had happened was that the untrained, poorly paid, demotivated work-force had gone on strike at the start of the third quarter and so hardly any of the customers' orders had been fulfilled.

Fortunately, this catastrophe occurred early on. Fortunately also, the MD, when he had got his act together, got his team's act together very rapidly. They uncovered the cause of the unpleasant effect, and his team went on to win by the proverbial mile. At the end, they had the best trained and best paid work-force ever!

Key Points

❑   This was a slightly artificial exogenous shock. Your team is unlikely to be running a business simulation in the workplace. Workplace exogenous shocks are a sudden "moving of the goal posts", the internal IT system crashing at a vital moment in a project causing a deadline to be missed, sudden loss of a key client – any unexpected event that impacts on the team's performance.

❑   The point is that the individual cannot help going down the reaction curve, with self-esteem reducing and the focus moving away from mutual support to meeting individual needs. The team becomes a collection of individuals and rapidly descends to the "conflict level" or "blood on the carpet" level.

❑   This is where you need to take control – not of the people, but of the process, i.e.

1.   Try to control your own emotions. Until you are in control of yourself, you have no hope of controlling the situation and building the team back to strong performance. You can use the *"cool pause"* or pauses already covered in Chapter 3 under the technique, "reflective listening".

2.   Acknowledge the team members' feelings, and point out the inevitable, temporary fragmentation of the team – the descent to

an overly individualistic and ego-centred state.

3. Suggest a "time-out" or "cooling off period".
4. Remind everyone (if you have no piece of plastic or prominent display) of the attitudes and actions to which every individual in the team has committed.
5. Then, you can lead a GDT session to develop solutions to the problem or problems that the exogenous shock has caused. If necessity is the mother of invention, in terms of sparking individual creativity, then GDT will solve any problem – even the mother of all problems.

ENDOGENOUS SHOCKS

❑   The most common endogenous shock is when a team-member "cocks-up", i.e. makes a mistake. If this is when the team is all together, there should be no problem at all, thanks to the "no blame" rule, which should be psychologically embedded by now, especially if you have ensured that the attitudes and actions have been prominently displayed. You could follow Brian Edward's strategy and get pocket laminates produced as well.

❑   The real problem occurs when the "mistake" takes place when the individual is working on his or her own, which will be the norm. Time for a true story entitled, "A wise investment". I heard it through the grapevine.

A WISE INVESTMENT
There was a manager working in a company, who made a very expensive mistake, as it cost the company over a million pounds. He told his boss, who, instead of being angry with him, said: "I have just invested a million pounds in your learning. I expect it to be a wise investment."

❑   You can now thank your lucky stars at your wise investment – building your staff into an effective team.

❑   Typically, in the workplace where "Conflict rules OK", the member of staff, who has made this costly mistake, will do everything in their power to cover it up. This is to avoid, "having his balls chewed off", or being instantly fired. Nick Leeson comes to mind, and look where that got Barings. I doubt he was ever part of a high-performing team!

❑ The alternative strategy adopted is to lay the blame elsewhere – on a fellow team-mate or a subordinate. This does not do very much for team dynamics.

❑ In your case, the member of staff, who has just had an unexpected "learning opportunity" presented to them, may come and tell you straightaway on a 1-1 basis, as well as having thought through beforehand and giving you all the possible solutions she or he can think of.

❑ Alternatively, the team-member may present the problem to the team to resolve, providing you have adopted the rule that any member of the team can call for a GDT session from those who are physically present – see note.

❑ If the team-member does come to you privately with solutions, then remember one of the basic rules you are all following is "sharing" and so call a team meeting ASAP to share the problem and receive the full benefits of GDT.

VARYING TEAM MEMBERSHIP AT MEETINGS

❑ The more the variation in membership at team meetings, the less chance of maintaining your now high-performing team. It is important, therefore, that you stress the need for every individual to place the highest priority on attending agreed meetings, and ensure you set an example. Fortunately, you are now in a virtuous circle.

❑ With the normal "conflict" meetings, everyone is trying to find an excuse not to attend the meetings, often telling porkies (my grandmother has died for the millionth time) or "persuading" some poor unfortunate to take their place.

❑ After the successful team-building workshop, everyone will be very keen to attend the next meeting and so they will, if they possibly can.

❑ However the reality of a hectic business life, when we have to do a host of tasks not related to the team we work for, and have to deal with the unexpected on a regular basis, means that there will be occasions when we will miss a meeting.

❑ The way to deal with this reality is to ensure you or the designated co-ordinator, if it is you that is absent, receive a full briefing of progress made by any absentee beforehand, preferably face-to-face, which is shared and discussed at the meeting.

❑ Equally, the absentee should be fully advised of the decisions taken at the meeting, including those that involve her or him in additional work. Consent should be obtained after the event by explaining the whys and wherefores.

❑ As you will be aware, formal minutes have or should have disappeared long ago. Key decisions taken and who does what, when is normally sufficient.

PERMANENT DEPARTURE OF TEAM-MEMBER

❑ These are the days of cost-cutting – becoming, "lean, mean, fighting machines", i.e. achieving more with less by working smarter rather than harder. The effective team is, of course, the smartest way there is to work.

❑ Not infrequently an intact team – whether board, departmental, functional, project or coal-face – has one of its members permanently removed, rather than replaced.

❑ This will put enormous strain on the team. There will be a fairly gradual descent to "conflict" as the group has bonded and can adjust more easily to the absence of a friend rather than the replacement by a stranger (see next section).

❑ In the absence of effective intervention by you, the remaining team-members, gripped by feelings of mutual support, will rush in to take on the extra work – but "conflict" beckons.

❑ Mistakes will be made, the team's performance will plummet, and some will find that they have bitten off much more than they can chew, and some will find that they have not actually got the technical skills or expertise to do the work they eagerly volunteered to take on.

❑ Clearly, there needs to be a team meeting to take a fresh look at task process, and ensure that the additional work falling on the team member is allocated fairly. This will usually mean transference of tasks between team-members, as well as the re-allocation of tasks previously carried out by the dearly departed.

– The chances are that only one or two individuals will have the technical skills or expertise required and will absorb the majority of tasks allocated.
– Unless they lose some of their existing workload to other team members, they will perceive themselves as being unfairly treated.

❑ All of this is not sufficient, because something else or a combination of something elses must also happen. Most people I know work hard and put in long hours. If all need to work harder and even longer, there will be too much stress on the team.

❑ So, ways need to be found out to ensure that overall hours worked do not increase. Some suggestions (and your team will probably come up with more if you GDT the problem) as a starter for ten are:

– Drop the least important work – the stuff that really does not need to get done by the team. In other words, carry out a re-prioritising exercise to gain greater focus on activities that are core to the team's success.
– Extend this re-prioritising to the work the individual does separate from the team and enable the individual to identify the relatively trivial and eliminate it.
– Abandon individual job descriptions and create new job descriptions that give team-work the primacy (given you can get more done faster) and reduce the amount of work the individual does that does not form part of the team projects.
– Use the opportunity to see if there cannot be a greater simplification of process, enabling the team and the individual to work smarter not harder. Take a case study – Zin cards:

ZIN cards

In November 1990, when I was still wet behind the ears and the recipe had not yet been developed, I was asked to be a support lecturer on the most popular programme we ran, which had the acronym PEM or Principles of Effective Management.

There was little attention paid to team-working, although there was a lot more working in teams than all our competitors. We were not an academic centre, but a down-to-earth pragmatic centre with lots of exercises and testing in teams.

I was put in charge of administrating the ZIN card exercise. There were a lot of cards, each containing a piece of information. The key to success (and therefore the learning point of the exercise) was the need to share information in the team in order to be effective and the need to appoint a co-ordinator to make that happen.

Typically, there was confusion, some conflict and then a rush to meet the deadline (just like the blindfold squares exercise with immature groups).

Typically, the groups failed or got there just in time. In this case there was just one right answer. The time given for the exercise was 30 minutes.

One team and only one team on the many occasions I managed this exercise stood out from the pack. I watched in awe as the team received the cards, information was absorbed and shared with incredible speed, only a few words were spoken and the right answer was produced in 12 minutes flat.

Another thing I noticed is that, normally, with each team, as each member had their own desk (in a team formation), there was quite a distance between each member. This team was already sitting very close to each other, before they were handed the cards.

Key Points

❑ Process can be an enabler for a team but it can also be a hindrance. We get stuck in process mode, following each step blindly and forgetting to think.

❑   This team had (and I don't know how) got into automatic pilot mode. In other words the team had become the expert – had absorbed the expertise of each individual and gone to a higher level.

❑   This comes with spending as much time as possible together as a single unit – so that is another strategy, which links into the previous point of making team-working the dominant work activity for the individual.

❑   Also, re-examine your processes, as you may have developed shortcuts or smarter ways of working that you have not consciously realised, and hold a GDT to consider how you can work smarter.

❑   It is possible that you have become too task focussed and not carried out reviews of individual and team performance, as set out in Chapter 8. Make these a priority and carry them out more regularly, as that will accelerate individual development and team performance.

❑   Introduce the rule that any individual can call a GDT session at the drop of a hat with those present – to help that individual team-member work smarter in their specific roles.

Author's note

We will cover the power of this rule in case study format, with the title: "The Power of Personal Experience".

The power of personal experience

In 1987, my boss was the Section Head (and a very left-brained individual – a Fellow of the Chartered Accountants) in Barclays Bank's Central Planning Department, I was the manager in charge of strategic planning, my colleague was in charge of special projects and we both had two junior managers reporting to us – Group High Fliers.

In 1986, I had attended the one-month General Management Development Programme, run by Ashridge Business School. For me, the most significant learning point was the first two rules of GDT (what "brainstorming" consisted of) and how you could develop creative group synergy as a result.

So I wrote my boss a lengthy, detailed paper (he was an introvert) setting out the *technique* and the *process* rules and how it would increase *efficiency, effectiveness* and *output*. [I must have intuitively used left-brained language, as I had not yet discovered the existence of and difference between left-brained managers and right-brained leaders.]

My boss agreed and I was appointed the process facilitator. In fact, my boss, unintentionally, when one of the junior managers put forward an idea, shrugged his shoulders and looked to the ceiling. I very politely pointed out his unintentional infringement of "no criticism by word or body language".

He accepted with good grace and never repeated this subconsciously driven infringement. [No boss likes to be "ticked off" by a subordinate and the fear of that happening again, coupled with his genuine conscious driver to "stick to the rules", a natural thing for him to do, successfully overcame his instinctive desire to criticise. With regular repetition of the new behaviour, a new habit formed and the positive implicit beliefs progressively removed the implicit negative limiting beliefs. He became a better person, and, no doubt, both his wife and two young children were delighted.]

The result of the successful application of the two first rules of GDT is that we became a high-performing team.

The Section Head was delighted with the increase in quality and quantity of output and the development of his own creating thinking skills.

The power of personal experience

As a result, we started socialising as a team, which had been singularly absent before, as well as making team-working much more dominant than before, where we had only had infrequent formal, fairly unproductive meetings. In fact, we started a system where each team-member invited the rest of the team to their homes to host a dinner party!

One of the rules we introduced is that any team-member could call all the team physically present together "at the drop of a hat" to help that individual with a particular problem or issue, applying GDT.

I was very grateful for this rule, as one project I was given was to produce a paper on how we could reduce overcapacity in banking. Within 15 minutes, the team had kindly provided me with my scoping paper.

Finally, I was responsible for the production of Barclays first long-term (10 year) strategic plan. One of the early tasks was to identify all the strategic issues facing the bank.

This would have taken me weeks and would have produced a lot of conflict with my boss, trying to get a left-brained boss to accept a load of right brained "twaddle".

The team spent a single day to achieve a far better result than I could have ever achieved working solo for 15 times as long.

❑ Finally, think seriously of making your boss the replacement, which leads neatly onto the next section.

CHANGE IN TEAM-MEMBER

❑ We are going to eavesdrop a conversation that took place amongst 12 Executives who had been split into 3 teams of 4 and had carried out a number of competitive exercises on land skis. The key determinant of success was the time taken going round the course. In the review session in the lecture room, they had just started to talk about the experience that one team-member of each team had had, when they had replaced a member of another team.

❑   I have given the name Mel to the coach, as it is fairly close to M&L.

Change and decay

"The next critical event was when I switched team-members. Let us ask those who switched teams how they felt about that, first of all?"

"Well, a bit uncomfortable," said Tony, who had moved from Alison's team to Peter's. We hadn't much time to plan. And, as soon as I arrived, I was told by the leader what their approach was, and what the verbal instructions were, and what place I should take up, which was different from where I was accustomed to, as I replaced the position vacated. I did my best in the run, though I made a few mistakes, and then went back to my own team with a hearty sigh of relief."

"My feelings and experience were similar", said Harry, and Joanna also agreed. Joanna and Harry were the other two, who had been displaced.

"And what was the result of this run?" asked Mel

Performance deteriorates

"Well, performance deteriorated for all the teams, quite markedly", Alison replied.

"So what is the conclusion?" continued Mel.

"If there is change in the composition of an effective team, the team performance will naturally deteriorate", came the quick reply from Tony.

"Agreed," said Mel. "Let us explore this a little bit further. Has anyone experienced a change in team composition in the recent past"?

"Yes, I have," said Joanna. "I had a multinational team – two Americans, a Brit, a German and Dane. We had been together for nearly a year and had developed into a very supportive, cohesive and focused unit, producing some excellent results. One American was promoted and replaced by a Dutch guy, Hans, and things started to fall apart. At our first meeting, very much a strategic brainstorming affair, Hans almost had a stand-up fight with the British woman. I chatted

Change and decay

with him afterwards, and he apologised, explaining that he profoundly disagreed with her views and felt he should express his own position. To cut a long story short, Hans never really settled in, and was sideways moved within a few months, much to the relief of the others, myself included, I am afraid to say."

"And what, in your judgment, were the reasons for this unsuccessful outcome?" queried Mel.

"First of all, I felt that I had been lacking in my leadership skills – I could have done better – which is one reason that I was so keen to come on this programme. Secondly, I thought there was just a personality clash – specifically that Hans had the wrong personality to fit into the team."

"Anyone else got a recent experience to relate in this area?"

"Yes," said George. "I too have a team, mostly American with one German and one Brit. It too developed into a united cohesive unit, and, also, one of the Americans was replaced with Jack, another American, as it happened. The problem was that Jack just wouldn't contribute in what had been a high octane, boisterous and busy environment. It was months before Jack started to actively contribute at team meetings – though now, to be fair, he is a fully integrated member".

"Thanks, George", said Mel. "Let's see if we can draw some concrete conclusions. First of all, we know that any new member joining an unfamiliar group will feel uncomfortable, is not going to be confident and competent, and the team's performance will suffer. If you like, if you have an effective team which obeys D'Artagnan's motto, "All for one and one for all", then once there is a replacement, that bond and the task focus is bound to be broken. To what extent do you see this as the consequence of individual personality – the personality of the stranger and the clash with established group norms of behaviour?"

Changing group dynamics not personality clashes

"It isn't primarily to do with personality, at all," replied Hermann excitedly. "All our three new team members felt similarly, and all the

Change and decay

teams' performance suffered. It is simply a function of group dynamics if you like. The role personality plays is to determine the nature of the negative response, from Hans quarrelling to Jack opting out."

"So what is the learning for leaders, facing a replacement of one of their team members with another?"

Do not integrate – create a new team that lives

"Go back to basics", suggested Zainol. "Treat the entire team as if it was new. Re-build, re-generate the vision, reconsider task process, and re-create the bonding. As effective team leaders, we don't try to integrate a new member into an old team, which has died; we integrate all members, including the new one, into a new team, which lives."

CHANGE IN TEAM LEADER

Perils of being the new leader

"Before we move on, a final question. Imagine that there was an effective, united team and one member left and you were the replacement. What is more, the member, who left was the leader. You are the new team-leader."

"I don't have to imagine, said Harry. "Everything is starting to fit into place, you know. Thank God I came on this programme. If we start at the theoretical level, the team-members will be naturally inclined to reject their new leader, but they have to be careful, as he is their boss, with all the appraisal and other powers that position brings. So they are likely to resist, try to undermine his authority, say "yes" when they mean "no" and act according to their inclination rather than their word.

They may well compare him behind his back very unfavourably with the old leader, whom they respected and who represented the happy past. From the leader's perspective, he won't know exactly what is going on, but will find himself thwarted and frustrated, will

Perils of being the new leader

find the changes he wants are not implemented when he wants or as well as he expects. He may well begin to dislike specific individuals, and be inclined to move more and more into command and control, as his attempts at a more open involving approach seem to have failed. That's the theory and my experience in the recent past."

"And there will be variations on that theme for all new leaders," continued Tarisha, "again not because of personality, but the power of group dynamics."

Look, listen and learn – then build a new team from scratch

"So what should effective leaders do in this situation?" asked Chew rhetorically. "I know", he continued, "Look, listen and learn, and then start to build a new team from scratch."

Key Points

❑ I was a joint programme director for the Senior Executive Development programme from early 1991 to late 1998, when I left Sundridge Park to run my own development business.

❑ There has not been a single executive that has not agreed with the policy of "Look, Listen and Learn". Typically, they suggest around 90 days or three months.

❑ I would suggest that you run your team-building session with your new team the week after you arrive.

❑ Finally AND CRITICALLY, if your team-members are new to you, as they will be when you are the new leader [and this applies to the situation if you were to become an RTB (Rapid Team-Builder) in the implementation of Project Omega – see final Chapter], you need to understand and cater for what happens, when a group of strangers meet for the first time.

❑ When a group forms, i.e. the individuals meet for the first time, the group will be at a low level of development – immature. The individuals will be in a new unfamiliar situation, and there will be a high degree of confusion due to the unfamiliarity and uncertainty, generated by meeting strange people in a strange place with a strange boss or facilitator.

❑ They will be concerned with themselves rather than with others and in meeting their own security needs. They tend to be closed – cautious, reserved and wary. Some may think positively about this new team, but will be impatient with the muddle and confusion – wanting structure and purpose, and annoyed at its absence.

❑ Others will want to be somewhere else, anywhere else, and will feel exposed and awkward. They will perceive the rest of their team members, and particularly the leader, who has caused this unpleasant situation, as hostile. There will tend to be little communication and lots of silences. People will be polite – on their best behaviour.

❑ There will be a psychological dependency on the leader or facilitator and it is the facilitator's/leader's behaviours and actions at this first, inevitably transitory stage of developing the group, which holds the key to the course that the group will take.

❑ Now you have been dealing with a team, where you all know each other, and you have explained why you are all there and there is no "confusion" stage and degeneration into conflict. You can successfully carry out the four steps to building a high-performing team.

❑ However, that will not always be the case in your career and certainly was not the case for me for all the development programmes or strategic away days/weekends that I have run.

❑ Without exception, I have opened the programme with the following two overheads:

1. YOUR CURRENT SITUATION
Having to deal with three changes

- Never been here before.
- Never worked with this group before.
- Never met Rupert before.

2. HOW DO YOU FEEL?
Current feelings and questions

- I don't want to be here.

- I don't know what is going to happen to me.
- I think I might make a fool of myself.
- Who is Rupert and what is he going to do to me?
- I feel worried, and I am not at ease.
- How on earth did I come to be in this team?
- Maybe, I'll give it a go – maybe not.
- Well, at least I'm not at work.
- I wish I was at work.

☐ Demonstrating immediate empathy has an instant positive psychological impact.
☐ I answer all the questions and then move swiftly to the third overhead and first group exercise. This is the contents of the overhead.

3. INTRODUCTIONS
Key Questions

- What are the three qualities you like most about yourself?
- What is an interesting fact about yourself that most people do not know?
- What is the most exciting thing that has happened to you?
- If you had an unexpected day off, what would you do?

Process

- Pair off or form a trio.
- Find out the answers to the questions from your colleague or, if a trio, A-B-C-A.
- At the end, introduce your colleague to the group as a whole.

Key Points

- Starts the "socialising process."
- Accentuates the positive.
- Focuses on the individual as an individual – no work-related questions, deliberately.

- The individual has to focus on a colleague rather than themselves and is "forced" to ask only open questions, which are at the heart of developing empathy with and promoting discovery in another person. This develops good habits – effective questioning and listening – early on.

❑ After covering house-keeping and other related matters, the next slide I put up is the following.

4. IMPACT OF WRONG ENVIRONMENT

"Japanese prosecutors have charged four men with beating to death a cosmetics company manager during a training course for up-and-coming executives in Nagaski", the newspaper Yomiuri Shim bun reported. *"Yukio Suzuki died after allegedly being repeatedly abused by four colleagues and six employees of the training centre. Course participants are restricted to four hours sleep a night and are screamed at and slapped if they fail to respond immediately to abstract themes,"* the report said.

❑ This leads neatly to the fact that we are going to create the opposite of that environment, that, by far, the best environment that can be created is one where the individual is part of a high-performing team, and thence onto the "attitudes and actions" exercise.

RESTING ON YOUR LAURELS

❑ Some teams, e.g. project teams, have a defined duration. Once the project is finished, the team is disbanded. If you are the RTB, then ensure that success is fully celebrated, hold a final meeting to agree whether the team should meet again as a unit in a social context to swap notes and experiences, and suggest individuals develop an action plan to "leverage" their expanded network in the future.

❑ However, many teams are "eternal" or at least long-term – such as departmental teams, business unit teams, functional teams, Board teams and so on. There will be shorter-term goals and objectives, often of an annual nature, which will become the focus of such teams.

❑ Once a given goal is achieved, the team becomes vulnerable. One reason is that you need different processes to achieve different objectives. As you have discovered, the process to complete a specific brief or task is different from the process to progress a strategic issue.

❑ If a team follows the wrong process to achieve a given objective, it is likely to fail and, as the result of a "blame game" that can develop, producing "blood on the carpet", what is termed the "storming" or "conflict" default position for most workplace teams. As mentioned above, you have completely, and as a fundamental key to success, bypassed by starting the four-step team-building process by ensuring the adoption of the attitudes and action of a high-performing team. To avoid such an unpleasant outcome, you apply the step 7 process questions to any objective.

❑ The other problem is that the new project may require new roles, a new set of technical skills and expertise outside the group. The team applies the same roles and same set of technical skills (and insufficient expertise) to the new project and promptly fails, against all expectations. A rush to conflict will follow.

❑ As the ten-step process model covers both these eventualities, you will have no problems. As said before, it is always worth reviewing process on a regular basis to see if you can improve it.

❑ Finally, successful teams produce outstanding performance, because they provide the perfect environment to stretch and fulfil the individual. Individuals in successful teams become hungry to learn, to be stretched more and to achieve more.

❑ This means that the horizons of the team need to continuously expand and you, as the RTB, need to ensure that projects selected are progressively more difficult, demanding and hence fulfilling.

❑ If you rest on your laurels, the team may rest in individual pieces once again.

Chapter 10
Manage Effective Feedback

INTRODUCTION

❑   I am always amazed at the awesome power of the feedback session. It makes me feel very humble. The degree of self-awareness and honesty from every individual is incredible. I should expect it, but it always takes my breath away.

❑   Here we set out how you, once you have built your group into a high-performing unit, can manage an effective feedback session with your team that will produce the same outcomes – a positive powerful uplift to individual and team learning, enabling both the individual and the team to reach levels of confidence and competence that would have been unimaginable, when they were simply part of an immature group.

❑   We look at the key questions:

– When to hold it?
– What questions to ask?
– What next?

WHEN TO HOLD IT?

❑   The team needs to have developed maturity and suffered some of the inevitable changes that will affect performance, and have been restored or restored itself to high performance.

– I used the words "restored itself" because of the truth of the saying by Jan Carlson of Scandinavian Airlines: *"An individual without information cannot take responsibility. An individual with information cannot help but take responsibility."*

– Now, I have no doubt that you will do a brilliant job when the inevitable crisis erupts. However, no man (or woman) is an island and you need to follow one of the key principles you have agreed to – "sharing".

– As mentioned earlier, you should hand out copies of this book to each team-member at the end of the workshop, with the suggestion that it is a priority to read the vital three Chapters 7 to 9.

❑ So you want to hold it after the team has produced a good result, e.g. completed one of the projects or achieved a significant milestone.

WHAT QUESTIONS TO ASK?

❑ Start with carrying out a review of the action plan you agreed at the workshop and then ask the question:

❑ In the light of the review of our action plan, what should we do, as a team, to improve our performance even more?

❑ As regards to the individual questions, these are:

– What are three strengths you have shown in helping the team perform so well?

– What can you can you do to build on those strengths and how can we help you?

– What is ONE area where you think you can improve, what can you do to ensure improvement and how can we help you?

❑ The open questions ensure that you are promoting discovery in the individual, i.e. they answer the questions for themselves, and there should a period of time – say fifteen minutes – for each individual to gather their thoughts and provide the answers.

❑ The individual ego is very fragile, and I found (after quite a lot of testing) that 3 positives and one negative was the right psychological balance to ensure that there was no damage done. "Accentuate the Positive".

❑ You will need, obviously, to appoint a co-ordinator to manage the feedback process.

❑ The order is important – one strength, followed by another strength, followed by the "improvement area" and finishing on a high – the final strength. I would recommend that you leave the best (strength) to last.

❑ Clearly, it is a round robin and the co-ordinator should lead by example. However, start the next round with a different person.

❑ It will be a very effective and powerful session and ensures continued growth for the individual and the team.

WHAT NEXT?
Let your collective hairs down.

SUMMARY
To summarise, you now know how to:

❑ Apply the recipe to suit your own personality and style.

❑ Ensure that the team returns rapidly to high performance, when faced with all the changes that could knock it down to the conflict level.

❑ Run a feedback meeting in a way that ensures continued growth for each individual and the team as a whole.

Chapter 11

Transform Your Company's Profitability

INTRODUCTION

❑ Quoting from Chapter 6, we have:

"There is only one right CSD – to deliver effective team-working throughout the company ASAP. This CSD focuses on the true means – the staff - and delivers maximum profitability at minimal cost.

> – Staff will operate in highly motivational, high performance work environments or cultures.
> – The team is the best vehicle by far to manage change successfully.
> – Staff will focus on the client and indeed "delight the client".
> – The delighted clients will provide, through repeat business, extensions and referrals (with zero marketing costs), the outstanding profitability that has been the goal, but unachievable reality, down the decades for all but a few CEOs."

❑ I have called the vehicle to deliver effective team-working throughout the company – Project Omega. The first letter of the ancient (and current) Greek alphabet is Alpha and the last letter is Omega – hence the title.

❑ Project Omega is not just relevant for companies but any organisation, enabling them to achieve their goals much more rapidly than currently the case, and, if applied to State education systems, transform the quality of learning and life for pupils.

❑ *"Research based, intellectually rigorous and honest, well-*

conceived and creative". John Vincent, the former Director of HR, Chardon Rubber, USA.

❑   In this last chapter, we set out:

– How to get Project Omega off the ground.
– Implementing Project Omega
– Education, Education, Education.
– Concluding key points.

HOW TO GET PROJECT OMEGA OFF THE GROUND

❑   As it is a companywide project, the ownership must come from the top – your managing director (MD) or chief executive officer (CEO), [and in the case of education, the Secretary of State for Education]. Their role is simply to communicate the project internally – all the whys and wherefores and the project plan for implementation.

❑   Someone in your company, if not you, needs to have applied the recipe to their team and produced the outstanding success that will result. Conviction convinces.

❑   Going through "the proper channels" (you are still working for an organisation where 'politically correct' behaviour is de rigueur) the success and rapidity of the recipe needs to be advised and their attention drawn to the section in Chapter 6 on " Critical Strategic Drivers" that "proves" that transformation of profitability will result.

❑   The prospect of transforming profitably lights up the eyes of every CEO or MD, especially in an era, where a significant part of the remuneration package the CEO receives is based on performance.

IMPLEMENTING PROJECT OMEGA
PRIOR PROJECT LAUNCH – 2 WEEKS

❑   The first step is for the CEO or Personnel Director to appoint the Project Leader and group. The Project Leader spends 4 hours building the group selected into a high-performing unit. Then, the now high-performing team, can look at how they should develop and implement Project Omega for their particular organisation.

❑ [Remember that anyone who receives the recipe should be provided with a copy of the book. They only need to read the last 4 chapters.]

❑ They then become the Project Steering Group as well as a collection of RTBs (Rapid Team Builders). This will be the "Head Office" team or central team.

❑ Only when this has occurred, and any modifications of the six phases (see next section) to suit the organisational structure and culture have taken place, does the CEO launch the project.

Author's notes

❑ The project is based on pyramid dissemination principles. So the first step, as covered, is that the central team, drawn from Head Office or, in the case of education, the Department of Education, is formed and developed into RTBs.

❑ They will be running what I call EG development days, where EG is short for Effective Group, to create teams of local RTBs. These are members of staff drawn from the local operating units, who will deliver the EG development day to the end users, whether the managers in the workplace or teachers in the classroom.

❑ If the company is a global one, with large overseas operations, it makes sense to run the project in parallel with separate Steering Groups and a project team to manage the logistics – see next section.

❑ If the company is mainly a UK operation, but operates on a regional basis, then the project can be run in parallel on that basis. {This would certainly hold for education, as the local authorities are separate autonomous units.}

❑ Regarding numbers of local RTBs, who attend centrally run EG development days or end users, [who will be running the four hour recipe only for their staff or pupils], attending the locally run EG development days, that is a matter for the Steering Group.

❑ I have successfully run the four hour recipe, completely solo, for the top 46 decision-takers (split into 7 teams of 6/7) of a newly-merged merged Insurance company and a Lloyds underwriting syndicate. They were attending a day and a half's strategy event. I overheard the Chairman remark to the CEO at the end: *"This is a fantastic result and exceeded all expectations. What is more, we did it ourselves, and avoided the use of teams of expensive external consultants."*

❏ I also ran a day and a half "symposium" for the Managing Partner and all the partners (54 in total split into 8 teams of 6/7) of the Banking department of a global law firm. The location was Chamonix. The location for the next symposium was Lake Como. They also "forced" me to go to Hong Kong (twice) and Bangkok (twice) to train their lawyers and support staff.

❏ The Steering Group(s) will know what is best for their organisation, but my suggestion would be as follows:

– Where the local area has up to 7 managers use one local RTB. If there are less than 4 managers, then merge with a bigger area.

– For 8 or more managers, use 2 local RTBs (sharing the workload and exposing the participants to different personalities and style). Obviously, for higher numbers of managers, always use 2 RTBs.

– For 8 to 14 managers, split into 2 teams.

– For 15-21 managers, one EG development day split into 3 teams of 4-7.

– For 21 to 42 managers, run two local events with 2 or 3 teams, size varying from 4-7.

– For larger operations with manager numbers exceeding 42, I would aim for the norm of three teams of 5 to 6, i.e. three-line whip for 18, knowing that you will get at least 15. I have found that the atmosphere is more electric with 3 teams as compared to 2.

– With a very large head office/local operation, each pair of local RTBs can comfortably run 4 events in the 2 weeks available to them.

– If we err on the safe side and assume an average attendance of 10 per programme, then two local RTBs can cover 40 managers, i.e. a ratio of 20:1.

❏ See the addendum at the end of this section for my suggestion as to how to cater for those managers, who cannot attend an EG development day during the project period.

❑ For managers, you can also read teachers.

PHASE 1 – PROJECT LAUNCH AND LOGISTICS (4 WEEKS)
The following key activities will need to have been completed:

❑ The MD or CEO communicates the project to all staff using all the communication media available – paper, electronic, intranet, video conferences and so on – in whatever time sequence is deemed appropriate. Remember that a 3 times repetition of key points will ensure memory retention and that short-term memory only lasts three weeks.

❑ The Steering Group produces the design of the EG development day, PowerPoint presentations, handouts and orders copies of the book. It is a day so that, after lunch, there is some input and discussion of the key material from the book drawn from Chapter 9 onwards (post recipe), as well as a Q&A session and review.

❑ One of the RTBs should build a group of suitable staff, perhaps drawn from members from each of the functional areas, to form the team to oversee management of the logistics. Specifically, this team will ensure:

– All the local RTBs have been selected.
– All the logistics for their attendance on their EG development day in phase 2 have been completed
– All the logistics to enable local events, to be run by the local RTBs in phase 4, are completed.

PHASE 2 – HEAD OFFICE RTBs RUN EG DEVELOPMENT DAYS FOR THE LOCAL RTBs (2 WEEKS)
We look at the number of Head Office RTBs required:

❑ Assuming that the Steering Group is the sole delivery team, the RTBs can all fly solo (as they are training the trainers and not the end users) and deliver 4 events each in phase 2.

❑ I would only run 16 events, with all the team of 6 or 7 involved on a rotation basis, thereby always having generous emergency cover.

❑ We can increase the average number of Local RTBs attending to 15, as they will be rather keen on being trained.

❑ So 16 events would create a total of 240 local RTBs trained, and a total number of managers to be trained of 4800.

❑ This caters for all but the largest of companies. However companies of larger size can simply create as many self-managing RTB delivery team or teams as necessary to accommodate the total number of managers to be trained.

❑ So if you move from one to three central delivery teams, double the average attendance figures (remember that an RTB can handle up to 8 groups of 5 or 6) then the number of managers trained becomes 28,800. With an average team size of, say 5, that is 144,000 staff.

❑ The whole process has inbuilt flexibility. The Steering Group of RTBs can create as many delivery teams as is required.

Author's notes

❑ This proves that any organisation, whatever its size, can complete Project Omega, well within 6 months.

❑ As mentioned, the Steering Group will know precisely what suits your organisation best and, as already covered, the first thing the Steering Group should do is redesign the whole project to meet the organisation's specific needs.

PHASE 3 – READING AND PREPARATION DAY FOR LOCAL RTBs (ANY DAY IN 1 WEEK)

The local facilitators may well want to redesign the PowerPoint presentation and material to reflect any local variations in culture and ways of working – and, of course, they need to read the relevant chapters of the book.

PHASE 4 – LOCAL RTBs RUN EG DEVELOPMENT DAYS FOR THEIR MANAGERS (2 WEEKS)

The local events will have been organised in phase 1, and so it is simply a matter of them being run successfully.

PHASE 5 – READING AND PREPARATION DAY FOR MANAGERS (ANY DAY IN 1 WEEK)

❏ Managers will need to read the book and decide how they intend to deliver the recipe to their staff to suit their own personalities and styles.

❏ There is no question of a PowerPoint presentation. We have a manager with his or her team in the work-place.

❏ He or she will simply operate for the four hours in a co-ordinating role. All that will be required is a separate room, table and chairs, coffee and tea, and a flipchart with pens and so on, as specified in Chapter 7.

❏ However, there is a critical point to make. If the manager has a team, including himself or herself, of more than 7, then the recipe will need to be delivered twice. That caters for up to 13 direct reports – two teams of 7. With 15 direct reports or more, there is no problem.

❏ The manager appoints 3 team-leaders and so trains up a team of 4, including himself or herself. Each of the team-leaders trains up 3 team-members, which including himself or herself, produces the minimum of 4 for effective team-working.

❏ 14 direct reports is the difficult number. The manager will need to run the workshop 3 times.

PHASE 6 – MANAGERS BUILD THEIR STAFF INTO HIGH-PERFORMING TEAMS IN 4 HOURS (1 WEEK)

CRITICAL POINTS FOR TEACHERS' CENTRAL RTB TEAM

❏ For teachers, of course, they simply need to split their pupils into groups of 5/6 and successfully run the session with a maximum of 6 groups.

❏ Also, care and attention will need to be paid to modify the material to the age of the pupil. *You can start in reception.* In all primary schools I have come across, there are very unsuccessful attempts to introduce ground rules in the reception class. They are unsuccessful, because the rules tend to be told rather than discovered, there is insufficient repetition, so that they never "sink in" and most importantly, there is no effective monitoring.

❑ Remember that children from the age of 4 upwards love the creative thinking scenarios.

ADDENDUM

❑ Inevitably, not all the managers will be able to attend during the project period. So one of the local RTBs should hold a mop-up EG development day or days, provided there are at least 4 managers attending each extra event.

❑ The Steering Group of RTBs should also hold such mop-up events centrally to cater for the fact that there will be less than 4 managers, who need an EG development day, in some of the local areas.

❑ An alternative to the above, of course, is for the manager(s) to read the book and then build up his or her team.

❑ During phases 3 to 6, which last 5 weeks, the Head Office RTBs act as Local RTBs for Head Office managers.

❑ You can make the judgement as how senior executives are covered. There are two key requirements:

1. All front-line managers are covered so that all employees are covered.
2. All senior staff, who run the organisation or manage the managers, need to have experienced the 4 hour recipe.

❑ The total number of weeks in the pre-launch and 6 phases is 2 + 4+ 2 + 1 + 2 +1 +1 = 13 weeks or about 3 months. Given that you have 6 months, and given that high-performing teams work both smarter and faster than an immature group of individuals, any organisation, whatever its size, will be able to have completed the project and will be reaping all the benefits within six months of commencement.

EDUCATION, EDUCATION, EDUCATION

❑ After the election of the Labour Government in 1997, I developed the first version of "Project Omega" for Education".

- ❏ Realising that I needed street cred before approaching the newly appointed Secretary of State for Education, I wrote to the then editor of TES (The Times Educational Supplement) explaining the recipe and how it could be applied to the State sector and revolutionise the quality and effectiveness of our education.

- ❏ She phoned me up and, after I had answered her penetrating questions to her satisfaction, she assigned a reporter, Katherine Orton, to come to observe a suitable programme.

- ❏ So I organised her attendance at the start of one of the management development programmes run for St Ives plc, having cleared it with the CEO Brian Edwards, who had already attended an earlier programme – leading by example. Incidentally, the delegates gathered together for lunch and the programme started at 2 p.m.

- ❏ I was scuppered by "empowerment". I had no realisation at the time that the TES was a left-wing paper and was the pioneer of the new politically correct language and behaviours.

- ❏ In the "good old days", if a newspaper editor phoned up one of his reporters and told that reporter to carry out a particular assignment – advising the why, when and how – that would be the end of the matter.

- ❏ I had fed back all the details of which programme, where and when to the editor, who had passed it on to Katherine Orton, with whom I had had no contact at all, until she phoned me at my office in Sundridge at 8 a.m. on the Monday the programme was due to run.

- ❏ She had to be "empowered". I failed and I could have done nothing at all about failing. As soon as she heard that I had not been a teacher and was not an educational expert, she withdrew from the assignment on the basis that if you were not an expert or a teacher, then, by definition, you could have nothing useful to say on the subject of education.

- ❏ Incidentally, this is a universally held mindset, as I have found when talking to my wife and older daughter – both teachers.

- ❏ Well I was shattered – but there was nothing I could do. I am a persistent sort of person. So I sent Project Omega for Education to the newly appointed Secretary of State. I got some dismissive reply from some official or other. I did not give up.

❑ I sent Project Omega for Education to successive Secretaries of State for Education. With the Coalition, I included the Prime Minister, Deputy Prime Minister, Michael Gove (The Secretary of State for Education) and his four ministerial colleagues.

❑ Golden Reality Rule 3 prevailed, which I only recently realised existed. Because of the overwhelming flood of e-mails and written communications to the "personal" e-mail and postal addresses of all the government ministers from Joe and Joanna Public, who have frequently been encouraged to communicate to the "listening governments", the minions have been told something along the lines of: *"If you ever let any communication from the great unwashed cross my desk, then you will be "let go" to spend more time with your family"*.

❑ I conclude this section with one of the papers that formed my submissions to the numerous Secretaries of State for Education.

THE BENEFITS OF INTRODUCING EFFECTIVE GROUPS INTO SCHOOLS

If kids from the age of 4 worked in effective groups (EGs), then the following benefits would accrue, looking first at national, then educational and then specific benefits for children, parents and teachers:

NATIONAL

"The ability to learn faster than your competitors may be the only sustainable advantage in the new millennium," Royal Dutch Shell.

The introduction of EGs would enable just that. Our children would learn faster than those in all other countries and we would produce the talent-based economy that politicians from all sides of the political spectrum have set as a vision without, hitherto, an effective strategy to turn the vision into reality.

EDUCATIONAL

Here we look specifically at classroom size, length of lessons, homework, selection and social skills.

Classroom size

The learning unit becomes the group (with the ability to change group composition, say, three times a term). Teachers could more easily accommodate 10 units of 5 than 15, 20 or 30 individuals. Classroom size is no longer an issue!

Length of lessons

❑ One of the bug-bears of the present system is the hourly lesson, with all the logistical implications and waste of time as children dash from one classroom to the next.
❑ Devoting discrete chunks of time to each subject (e.g. mornings or afternoons) would reduce these logistical problems and time wasting as well as increasing the ability to make significant progression in the much longer lessons.

Homework

Homework becomes unnecessary because more subject matter is covered much more quickly and more effectively. In secondary education, the working week could be extended until 5 pm as in many continental countries. The absence of homework has three significant benefits:

1. It allows the child to relax and unwind, and to develop relationships and outside hobbies and interests.
2. It means that no child, who has parents who are indifferent or too busy to be involved, is disadvantaged,
3. It enables all parents to have happier relationships with their children and more time for themselves.

Selection

Because of the power of the approach to change individual potential into actual, there is no need for narrow banding on the basis of measured IQ. Instead the banding can be much wider with a greater mix of ethnic and social backgrounds – taking a great deal of heat, cost and pain out of education.

Social Skills

As Romiszowski found, the EG approach develops the creative, intellectual, and social skills of the individual, as well as helping to produce more rounded personalities. All these are highly significant benefits and over time can create the kind of value-based society that hitherto we can only dream about.

SPECIFIC BENEFITS

We conclude the paper by looking at the specific benefits for children, parents and teachers.

Children

Our children would enjoy going to school! They would enjoy being part of productive teams and not unproductive gangs. Bullying would die out, and no child would find themselves isolated or lonely. Academic standards would soar and those who chose further education would increase at a rapid rate.

Parents

The quality of life would improve significantly, as would the relationship with each child. No more guilt feelings at not helping sufficiently with homework because of busy careers, no more trying to persuade recalcitrant boys to buckle down to homework when they want to play with their mates!

Teachers

The teacher has a much more positive relationship with pupils, a more relaxing time in the classroom, and only has to mark the official tests!

CONCLUDING KEY POINTS

❑   I hope you have found this book very useful. Not only should it enable you to develop WINNING WAYS TO WORK, but, as nearly all the insights, learning and skills you will have developed are transferable to all walks of life, it will help you to be a winner in your home and in social environments.

❑   If you do, then please feel free [nay I would positively encourage you to "care and share"] to spread the good news.

❑   Please twitter away, blaze in your blog, flood your Facebook and exercise your e-mails!

Have a great life

Rupert

P.S.

Ever since 1997, I have "had a dream" – that "Project Omega" for Education is implemented in the UK and then spreads around the globe. I hope my dream comes true before I shed my mortal coil. If you could also use all the above media and any personal contacts you may have to get this book read by whomsoever happens to be the Secretary of State for Education, that would be absolutely fantastic.

www.legendpress.co.uk

www.twitter.com/legend_press